THE PATH

THE INNER LIFE OF JESUS CHRIST

THE
PATH

THE INNER LIFE OF JESUS CHRIST

GEOFFREY S. CHILDS

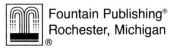
Fountain Publishing®
Rochester, Michigan

DEDICATION

To our friends in South Africa

THE PATH

Published by Fountain Publishing®
P.O. Box 80011, Rochester, Michigan 48308-0011
www.fountainpublishing.com
in cooperation with the General Church Publication Committee

Printed in the United States of America by Fidlar Doubleday, Inc.
Book Design by Lisa Alfelt Eller
Cover art © 2001 by Kären Childs Elder
Second Printing

Childs, Geoffrey S, 1926-
    The Path: The Inner Life of Jesus Christ/ Geoffrey S. Childs

ISBN 0-9659164-6-4

ACKNOWLEDGEMENTS

I would like to thank Keith Morley, the Rev. Erik Sandstrom, Sr., David Childs, and my wife Helga for their advice and support. Without them this book would not have been completed. I would also like to thank Don Fitzpatrick, Dr. Bob Gladish, Vera Glenn, and the Rev. Doug Taylor for their careful work in editing the manuscript. Also, I thank the editors at Fountain Publishing for focusing this book more specifically on the Lord's inner life. Their encouragement and affection for the subject matter are deeply heartening. In particular I would like to thank Karin Alfelt Childs for her careful scholarship and sensitive perceptions.

NOTE FROM THE AUTHOR

The Theological Writings of Emanuel Swedenborg are quoted and referred to throughout this book as the source for much of the information about the inner life of Jesus. However, these Writings do not tell of the Lord's inner life in a continuous way, because they also refer to the life of human beings and to churches. So from study and reflection, I have filled in some gaps. With the same approach I also have matched descriptions of the Lord's inner life with known incidents in His life on earth.

TABLE OF CONTENTS

INTRODUCTION

"For if you believed Moses, you would believe Me, for he wrote about Me" (John 5:46).

The New Testament is silent about much of Jesus' life as an infant and child. What was happening then? What was He experiencing?

We are all aware of the Christmas story: the promised birth of John the Baptist, the annunciation to Mary, the Lord's birth in Bethlehem. We know that first the shepherds came to adore Him and that later the magi from the East arrived with their gifts. We recall that shortly after the wise men left, Joseph was warned in a dream by night to flee into Egypt with Mary and the infant Jesus.

How old was the child Jesus when He left Egypt? What did He learn there? We know only that when it was safe, Joseph, Mary, and Jesus returned to Canaan. Joseph by-passed Jerusalem because he feared Archelaus who now ruled there as successor to his father, Herod. The family went back to Nazareth.

What happened between the time that the Lord returned to Nazareth and the time that He was twelve years old? These are vital years in His growing up, but again we know nothing about them from the gospels. At age twelve, Jesus traveled with Joseph and Mary down to Jerusalem so that the family might observe the Passover feast. On their journey home, Joseph and Mary realized that Jesus was not with the caravan. They rushed back to Jerusalem and sought frantically for Him for three days. Finally they found Him in the temple, speaking and listening to the teachers there and showing wisdom that "astonished" those who heard Him.

The next time we hear of Jesus, He is thirty. Eighteen years have passed. What happened during these years? It seems that the Lord had stayed in Egypt for about three years before returning to

Nazareth with Joseph and Mary. If this is accurate, nine years passed in Nazareth between the ages of three and twelve. Nine years and eighteen years – twenty-seven years of Jesus' life, and of these we know next to nothing from the New Testament.

For believing Christians this is one of the mysteries of the Bible. Obviously these were vital years in His development. We are told that He "increased in wisdom and stature, and in favor with God and men" (Luke 2:52). We are also told in Mark (6:3) that He took up the trade of carpentry: "Is not this the carpenter?"

These gaps in the history of the Lord's life on earth have led to many legends. Some say He went to the lost tribes of Israel; others that He traveled to the Orient and taught there. But these are simply guesses. There is no conclusive evidence.

During His ministry on earth the Lord promised that He would disclose more.

"I still have many things to say to you, but you cannot bear them now. However, when He, the Spirit of Truth, has come, He will guide you into all truth" (John 16:12,13).

On the walk to Emmaus with two of His followers on Easter afternoon, the Lord responded to their terrible anxieties:

"Ought not Christ to have suffered these things, and to enter into His glory?" And beginning at Moses and all the Prophets, He expounded to them in all the Scriptures the things concerning Himself (Luke 24:26,27).

Later these two followers said, "Did not our heart burn within us while He talked with us on the road, and while He opened the Scriptures to us?" (Luke 24:32)

What did Jesus tell them? Did He reveal how, within the Old

Testament, Moses and the Prophets speak about His own life on earth?

Later in Luke we read that Jesus also unfolded the Scriptures to His disciples on Easter evening. He said to them,

"These are the words which I spoke to you while I was still with you, that all things might be fulfilled which were written in the Law of Moses and the Prophets and the Psalms concerning Me." And He opened their understanding that they might comprehend the Scriptures (Luke 24:44,45).

He told them the things written within the Old Testament concerning Himself. Somehow, the books of Moses, the Psalms, and the Prophets teach of the Lord's life on earth. If they speak of His states and education and experiences here, do they tell us what happened during those missing years?

I believe that the Lord's answers to these questions are in the Theological Writings of Emanuel Swedenborg. From these works, called by many simply "The Writings," we learn that within the stories of the Old Testament lie hidden stories which treat of the Lord's lifetime on earth in great depth and detail. But the Old Testament does not treat of the Lord's outer history – the day-by-day outward events of His life. Rather, it deals with His inner history, that is, His loves and His struggles, and the development of His mind and character. This highest "sense" or meaning in the Bible tells of the successive mental states of His infancy, childhood, youth, and then His entire life on earth.

But before relating the inner story of Jesus Christ, I will first treat of what Jesus Christ came on earth to achieve. Why, indeed, did "the Word become flesh"? (John 1:14)

The young virgin Mary was at first frightened and bewildered by the appearance of the angel Gabriel, announcing that she would give birth to the Savior of humankind. And yet, despite being unable to fully understand what this event would mean, she answered willingly from her heart: "Behold the maidservant of the Lord! Let it be to me according to your word" (Luke 1:38).

By this willingness, Mary was able to serve God, but not only by providing a mother's arms to hold and care for the infant Jesus. By coming through a finite human mother, Jehovah God was able to inherit both a material body and all the finite tendencies and weaknesses that make human beings vulnerable to evil. Though Mary herself was sweet and good, she held within her, as all finite humans do, the imperfections that can allow a person to be led astray.

Only by means of such a birth could Jehovah God come all the way down to the level at which humans were struggling. Though Jesus visibly cast out many demons during His life on earth, this was only a glimpse of a much larger picture. The influence of evil spirits from hell on human hearts and minds had swelled tremendously. The cruelty and ignorance that the hells were inspiring threatened to cut off all contact between humankind and its God. And so Jehovah came down to us as Jesus, born into the human condition through a finite human mother. Only there could He dwell with us, to face the pain and confusion and ignorance that had been attacking the human race. Only there could He work to confront these hellish forces, and forge a path back to love, wisdom and peace which we can follow after Him.

Emanuel Swedenborg, an eighteenth-century scientific genius, was prepared during the first part of his life to become a scribe through whom the Lord would reveal "the Spirit of truth." In 1748, after a powerful vision of Christ, Swedenborg was divinely inspired to write a series of books about the deeper meanings contained within the stories of Genesis and Exodus. These books are entitled *Arcana Coelestia* (abbreviation AC) which in Latin means *Heavenly Secrets*.

The *Arcana* begins by describing the inner meaning or "internal sense" of the stories of creation: Adam and Eve, Cain and Abel, Noah and the flood, and the tower of Babel. For instance, in the internal sense the stories of creation are the stories of our spiritual creation - of our regeneration, or rebirth, in seven "days" or seven major stages.

But then, in describing the inner meanings in chapter twelve of Genesis, the *Arcana* takes on a new focus. It begins to tell the story of the Lord's life on earth, from His birth and first infantile awareness to the completion of His Divine mission. This is revealed in the inner meaning of the stories of Abraham, Isaac, Jacob, and Joseph.

ABBREVIATIONS

Abbreviations of the theological Writings of Emanuel Swedenborg used in this volume:

AC	*Arcana Caelestia* (or *Arcana Coelestia*)
TCR	*True Christian Religion*
Lord	*Doctrine of the Lord* (Part of "The Four Doctrines")
SE	*Spiritual Experiences*
CL	*Conjugial Love* (sometimes translated "True Marriage Love")
Life	*Doctrine of Life* (Part of "The Four Doctrines")
AE	*Apocalypse Explained*
Ath. Cr.	*The Athanasian Creed*

All number references in the text refer to paragraphs, not pages, in conformity with Swedenborg's own numbering system.

Most references to the Writings are from Swedenborg Foundation standard editions of *Arcana Coelestia* (John F. Potts translation, New York, 1949). The exceptions are volumes of *Arcana Caelestia* from The Swedenborg Society editions (John Elliot translation, London, 1983), which I used in addition to the Swedenborg Foundation standard edition volumes.

The Bible quotations from Genesis are taken from the above translations of Swedenborg's works. Other Bible quotes are taken from the New King James Version (Copyright 1979, 1980, 1982 by Thomas Nelson, Inc.).

GLOSSARY

Some terms used in certain translations of Swedenborg's works.

Ancient Church = religion of the people of ancient times, represented by Noah and his descendants

Celestial = supremely heavenly; having a quality of highest goodness and love (the quality of loving the Lord)

Celestial of the spiritual = 1. heavenly and loving qualities on the spiritual level; 2. good qualities that come from living according to true beliefs from love

Charity = love of the neighbor

Cognition = items of knowledge relating to interior things

Conjugial love = the love in a monogamous marriage of souls, minds, and bodies

Correspondence = the relationship between things on two different levels of reality, usually the spiritual and the physical

Evil spirit = an evil person in the world of spirits

Glorification = being exalted to glory (the process by which Jesus became Divine)

(The) hells = a collective reference to evil people in the spiritual world

Mediate good = goodness that is not genuine but is allied to what is genuine and is useful

Merit = taking credit or glory for achievements (in Swedenborg's works, often used to describe taking credit for something in which credit really belongs to God)

Most Ancient Church = the most ancient religion in which highest love and perception ruled, represented by Adam and Eve

Natural = belonging to nature; worldly; earthly (in contrast with "spiritual")

Proprium = what is one's own; self; selfhood, the feeling of self

Regeneration = the lifelong process of being spiritually reborn, and of becoming an angel

Remains = good loves and thoughts that are deeply impressed on the inner part of a person and "remain" with him (the most significant of these are acquired in infancy)

Sensuous = involving the senses; physical sensation; the part of the mind that draws evidence and experience from the senses

Spiritual = 1. belonging to the spirit (with special emphasis on the quality of truth in contrast to "celestial" which is a quality of goodness and love); 2. not natural; not external; higher level than the natural

Spiritual of the celestial = truth that comes from celestial goodness

Most of these definitions are drawn from *Words in Swedenborg and Their Meanings in Modern English* by Frank Rose (General Church Press, 1985).

Chapter One

The Birth and Infancy of Jesus

The Call of Abram
Genesis 12, verses 1-7

+ **Jehovah tells Abram to leave Haran.**

+ **Abram takes his wife and family to Canaan.**

+ **Jehovah appears again to Abram, promising the land of Canaan to his descendants.**

+ **Abram builds an altar to Jehovah.**

To read about Genesis chapter 12 in the *Arcana Coelestia* of Swedenborg is to discover a new world, for one finds, as if by a Divine miracle, that Abram's life viewed from within is the story of the Lord's infancy, childhood, and youth. The lives of the following patriarchs — Isaac, Jacob, and Joseph — represent later stages in His life on earth. They reveal His adult states or frame of mind, leading up to the final temptations, His crucifixion, and the glory of Easter.

The infant Jesus' first mental awareness is represented by Jehovah's appearing to Abram and calling him out of Haran to a land that "I will cause you to see."

Genesis 12 says:

"And Jehovah said to Abram, 'Go away from your land,

and from the place of your nativity and from your father's house, to the land that I will cause you to see. And I will make you a great nation. . . .' And Abram went as Jehovah had told him. . . .And they came to go into the land of Canaan; and into the land of Canaan they came" (Gen. 12:1-5 passim).

Abram directly symbolizes or represents the Lord Jesus Christ, here as a newborn infant. Who is this child? He is a person unique in the history of the earth. He is Jehovah, Who "bowed the heavens and came down" (Psalm 18:9) to be born of a virgin mother. This child's Soul is Divine, for it is Jehovah Himself. But the body He assumes from Mary is finite and human. His heredity is unique in being Divine from the Father and human from the mother.

Between the soul and body stands the mind, and it is affected by each. What kind of mind will this child have? As a tiny babe in the manger at Bethlehem, He is like any other infant in outward appearance. He is innocent and helpless, needing love and care. But inwardly He is a Wonder Child. Gabriel announces His birth to the shepherds, and the heavenly hosts sing with joy. They know this is Jehovah, born on earth, and that He has come to save humankind, a people suffering in misery.

In the stories of the Word of God or Bible, any place or city represents or "corresponds" to a state of mind, or to affections and thoughts. The infant Jesus is born in Bethlehem of Judea. Why is Jesus born in this tiny Judean village? The Writings of Swedenborg respond:

"The reason why the Lord was born in Bethlehem and not elsewhere is that He alone was born a spiritual-celestial man, but all others are born natural, with the capacity to become either celestial or spiritual by regeneration from the Lord" (AC 4594).

"Spiritual" refers to things concerned with the spirit, with a special emphasis on the quality of truth. "Celestial" refers to even deeper, more heavenly aspects of the spirit, which have to do with

20

goodness and love. We humans are born "natural," meaning that our first concerns have to do with worldly and physical things. We have to learn and grow to achieve appreciation of things of the spirit. The Lord, on the other hand, is born a "spiritual-celestial" person and Bethlehem symbolizes a spiritual-celestial state of mind. "Spiritual-celestial" describes an ability to experience heavenly qualities of love, touched by an enlightened understanding.

In His inner mind Jesus is born with a love for the salvation of humankind: this love is celestial (AC 2034, 2077, 1434). With this love comes a spiritual inborn and intuitive ability to perceive truth. Being born spiritual-celestial is a gift given to the infant Jesus Christ alone. He is born with the love of rescuing us and is open to perceptions about how to do this.

Where did this spiritual-celestial quality come from? The Word says, "He bowed the heavens and came down" (Psalm 18:9). That is, His Soul implanted in this infant's mind the loves and wisdom of the angels of the highest heavens (see AC 6371). He is born angelic in the inner level of His mind.

This blessing of the spiritual-celestial in Jesus is from His Soul, but this is hidden deeply within. He gradually becomes aware of its power and depth as He grows, as He fights the hells and conquers. Most of the time as He is growing up, Jesus' awareness is on this plane that is called His "human essence," which is His spiritual-celestial nature.

From this plane of awareness Jesus reaches up to His Soul. Gradually this human essence, his love for saving humankind, matures, deepens, and draws nearer and nearer to the Divine Love of saving souls that is within Him. Jesus longs to become One with His Soul, His Father. In this He is uplifted also by the angels, for the celestial kingdom is within Him. But in the human part of His heredity that He received through Mary, a finite human mother, He has to combat inclinations toward the same hellish desires that we finite humans have to fight.

Jesus is a child born with pure love. How this love is developed is revealed in the inner meaning of Genesis as it unfolds the complete story of Abraham's life.

The infant Jesus' first awareness is unlike that of any other child. With other infants this first awareness is a sense impression, perhaps of the mother or of being fed, tied to an innocent willingness to be led. With the infant Jesus, His first awareness is that He is living in the level of sensing things with His body. There now comes a call to leave these lower things and to ascend to heavenly love. His higher mind is urging the infant to ascend to love itself, even to love for serving humankind. This is represented by **Jehovah's call to Abram, telling him to leave Haran and travel to Canaan** — to leave lower things and to ascend to celestial love.

This call is almost incomprehensible (AC 1414). Can a tiny infant feel such desire to love? Only when His Soul is Divine and His infant mind is like the angels'. This call to Abram symbolizes an inner voice calling to Jesus, urging Him upwards.

In the New Testament nativity story this may be symbolized by the circumcision and naming of the child "Jesus." Circumcision represents the removal of evil desires (AC 2039), and the promise of regeneration or rebirth. For the infant Jesus, circumcision represents a Divine call to leave corporeal or bodily things and ascend to love itself, even to the Divine itself. Most deeply, it is a call to become Divine.

Jesus' circumcision stirs the heavens with hope; it is the promise that He will be the Savior, the Rescuer of humankind from its desperately fallen state.

Jesus responds to Jehovah's call, leaving lower bodily things and traveling toward the celestial itself. We read in Genesis 12, **"and into the land of Canaan they came" (Gen. 1:5).** This represents that Jesus "attained to the celestial things of love" (AC 1438). Canaan represents heaven and also represents the Divine as the origin of all things. The infant Jesus was looking upward to Divine Love.

The celestial things of love are the inmost keys to life. Every infant is surrounded by celestial states of innocence and of love toward the Lord. Infants live in a garden of love where the best things of life are implanted without knowledge being involved. These are the innocent qualities called "remains". Feelings of love and peace "remain" hidden within us our whole lives. These "remains" are protected, and are awakened in us by the angels at various times in our lives. Remains enable us to be truly human and to shun evil as adults, and be saved. Gifts from the Lord and our link to heaven, they go back to a time when we are not even aware of evil. This term "remains" (or "remnants") for the innocent states of infancy is found especially in the early *Arcana* (AC 8, 1906, 1555 et al).

The Lord as an infant also comes into celestial states of mind, but with Him they are of a unique quality. For together with the celestial angels who are present with all other infants, the baby Jesus has the Divine Soul Itself present, for the celestial Seed is within Him.

This infant is specially endowed and Divinely protected. Imagine how the hells lust to attack and destroy Him in these earliest states. But they cannot. They cannot even approach closely, for the Divine Soul protects Him.

At the same time, this infant has inherited tendencies to evil. In this early innocent state these are quiescent, but they are present in His external heredity received through His mother. In Divine order this must be so, for the Lord was born on earth to meet the hells in combat, and they need to have access to Him. This is represented by the phrase: **"and the Canaanite was then in the land"** (AC 1444).

"And Jehovah appeared to Abram. . . and there he built an altar to Jehovah Who appeared to him" (Gen. 12:7). It would follow from the whole purpose of the life of Jesus that Jehovah would appear to Him (see AC 1445). The altar Abram built is Jesus' initial worship of Jehovah.

What an awe-inspiring experience this is for the infant Jesus. His Soul, Jehovah, the God of all creation, appears to Him. His reaction is one of intense love and of worship. The appearing may well have been through an angel, but the Soul, the Divine Love, shines through this angel. This vision is not a matter of intellectual realization with Jesus; it is a vision seen and perceived by His infantile heart (AC 1464).

Perhaps in the New Testament this vision happened at the time of the presentation of the infant Jesus in the temple at Jerusalem on the fortieth day. This temple is a symbol of Jehovah. To bring Jesus to the temple is a picture of Jesus coming into the presence of His Soul, Jehovah. The sacrifice made then by Mary and Joseph parallels the worship of Abram at the altar.

Every infant experiences a state corresponding to the appearing of Jehovah to Abram. The sensations of an infant are said to come together in time to form the first clear, conscious concept. In most cases this would be a concept of the mother who feeds and nourishes the newborn. Highest celestial affections center on this awareness of the mother who stands in place of God. This is deeply moving to the infant and forms the basis of future concepts of and love for the Lord Himself. It is one of the most powerful moments in human life, secret and hidden though it is, and its importance is hard to overstate. The call of Abram out of Haran finds in this awareness its completion in each human being.

With Jesus Christ the call and the awareness of Jehovah are of great clarity, for in His case it is Jehovah God Himself who appears. This is unique. It is a preparation for His Divine mission.

Chapter Two

THE EARLY EDUCATION OF JESUS CHRIST

ABRAM'S TRAVELS
GENESIS 12, VERSES 8-20

> ✦ Abram and his family journey to Bethel.

> ✦ Then they journey further, to the south.

> ✦ Later, because of a famine, they go to Egypt.

Abram left Shechem in Canaan and journeyed to the mountains east of Bethel. These mountains represent further states of love the infant Jesus experiences and the light that comes from this love. **Abram then traveled toward the "south" (Genesis 12:9).** The south represents a state of wisdom. Within Himself the Lord now starts moving toward wisdom, and this for the first time in His earliest life (see AC 1457). He is to advance into learning knowledge and then into wisdom, and this will be a lifetime process.

The New Testament story implies that after Jesus is presented in the temple, Joseph and Mary return with Him to Bethlehem and there find a home in which to live. There the wise men from the east come to find the babe. They "fell down and worshiped Him. And when they had opened their treasures, they presented unto Him gifts: gold, frankincense and myrrh" (Matt. 2:11). These gifts represent their love, faith, and obedience.

The wise men are among the last people of an Ancient Church, and they know Who this child is. In laying down their gifts, they express awe together with humility and adoration. Their actions are especially appropriate at this time, for now the infant Lord is just starting His journey into wisdom. The coming of the wise men to the child may parallel Abram's journeying toward "the south."

After the wise men leave, the angel of the Lord appears to Joseph "in a dream, saying, 'Arise, take the young child and His mother, flee into Egypt, and stay there until I bring you word' " (Luke 2:13). So also, Abram traveled down into Egypt. **"And there was a famine in the land; and Abram went down into Egypt to sojourn there, for the famine in the land was serious" (Gen. 12: 10).** With the infant Jesus the famine is a lack of knowledge, or of clear cognitions. Cognitions are knowledges relating to interior or spiritual things. He is also openly threatened by Herod's wrath, which expresses the animosity of the hells.

Jesus is in a state of deep hunger for instruction and for inner cognitions. His Soul and angel-like mind exert strong influence, and the infant, young as He is, is ready to learn. He has precocity far beyond that of any child genius who ever lived (see AC 1464).

This superior genius is without conceit. Instead, He is love itself, a love of others more than of self. How touching it would be to know Him then, a being of unselfish love and yet of incomparable genius. Mary and Joseph are deeply moved and affected by Him, as all caring parents are by the sphere of innocence around their infants (see CL 395). But with the infant Jesus, His Soul is Innocence itself.

Abram's traveling down into Egypt and "sojourning" there represent the Lord's instruction and gaining knowledge from the Word of God. This Word exists in the Old Testament and in an older

Ancient Word[1], as well as other ancient knowledge, including the hidden symbolism in nature itself. For Egypt symbolizes knowledge and cognitions. The child Jesus wills to learn only from the Word, for this was opened for Him to its highest level, where Jehovah is (see AC 1461).

The Lord is very young when He begins to receive this instruction. His special genius and His purpose for being on earth make this possible. How wonderful it must be for this infant-child to start to learn from the Old Testament in ways we never dream of. Many levels of meaning would be opened up to Him by His Soul. He also learns from "correspondences" which are hidden spiritual causes and meanings of natural objects. This is an ancient knowledge that the first people on earth used in a Golden Age long ago, and the angels learn in this way even today (AC 1805-1808).

How the child Jesus learns, in an outward way, we do not know. We are not told how He is taught to read. We do know that He learns from the Word of God alone. He learns in order that He may love more effectively — to inform fully His burning love for the salvation of humankind. Yet at the same time, He is only a child, and He has some of the limitations of other children.

One limitation Jesus shows is that He becomes almost enraptured by the wondrous cognitions and knowledge He is learning (AC 1495). He loves these concepts for the visions and joys that they bring Him. For a time He becomes unaware that He is learning for the sake of uplifting others. This happens in Providence from His Soul, so that He learns this wonderful knowledge with great swiftness and eagerness. But later He is made aware that He must rise above loving this knowledge merely for the sake of the delight that it gives Him. He must yield up that delight to a higher one, a delight

---

1. A written revelation that existed among the Ancients before the Israelitish Word. Moses was acquainted with this Ancient Word. From it He acquired the symbolic stories of creation, Adam and Eve, Noah, and the Tower of Babel. Moses also refers to portions of the Ancient Word in Numbers 21:14, 15, 27-30, and references are made in 2 Samuel 1:17, 18 and Joshua 10:12,13 (cf. TCR 264-266)]

in learning for the sake of loving others. Knowledge is not an end in itself but a means of showing kindness to others out of genuine love. The Lord now learns this, and perceives it in His heart.

He feels "grief" at this loss of delight in sheer knowledge. Nevertheless, He makes this sacrifice and comes instead into a far higher and more delightful state of the deepest love for others (AC 1492, see also AC 1462:6).

ABRAM AND LOT SEPARATE
GENESIS 13

> ✦ **After the famine, Abram and his family return to Canaan.**
> ✦ **The herdsman for both Abram and Lot, Abram's nephew, fight over the land.**
> ✦ **Once Lot has left, Jehovah shows Abram the land and promises the land to him and his descendants.**

After the famine eased, Abram and his entire family went up out of Egypt and returned to the land of Canaan. So too, after Herod dies, the child Jesus leaves Egypt and returns to Canaan.

Biblical scholars estimate that Jesus was taken up out of Egypt at about age three. They use the approximate time Herod died and was succeeded by Archelaus as the basis for their estimate. We don't know when the Lord's actual state of special focus on gaining knowledge, represented by Egypt, comes to a conclusion. One would think He is far older than three years, but we judge by our own finite concepts of mental progress. Certainly the Lord as a boy goes on learning while in Nazareth, but the level of learning then is on a celestial or inmost plane rather than the lower plane symbolized by Egypt.

As a young boy in Nazareth, the Lord experiences heavenly states. The *Arcana* says of Abram traveling back up to Canaan:

"Described here is the state of His external man as it existed in childhood when it was first endowed with facts and cognitions — how it moved on from these more and more towards conjunction with the Internal" (AC 1536).

The "external man" is the Lord's conscious awareness as a boy; the "Internal" is His Soul, Jehovah — the God of all creation. As He draws nearer to His Divine Soul while a young boy, He leaves Egypt and enters into "celestial light" — the light of innocent love. This is represented by the phrase **"Abram went up. . .toward the south,"** the "south" symbolizing celestial light.

Although the Lord draws closer to His Soul, He is still only a boy in many ways, and "worldly things" are present with Him (AC 1557). These are not actual evils — the Lord never had actual evils — but they are worldly interests. We can picture Him then as a young boy in Nazareth, in appearance like other boys, but filled with a tender celestial love (AC 1545) and having a unique strength and perception.

That **"there was strife between Abram's herdsmen and Lot's herdsmen"** and that **"the Canaanite and the Perizzite were then dwelling in the land"** represent hereditary evil tendencies present in Jesus inherited through His mother (AC 1573:3). To face and conquer the hells the Lord needs to experience temptations, and the hells have access to Him through His inherited tendencies that were taken on by being born to a finite human mother.

Lot symbolizes Jesus' outer consciousness or sensory awareness (see AC 1541), that is, His awareness from His bodily senses. This is at the early stages of Jesus' learning process, and He is indeed very young. "Herdsmen" or shepherds symbolize "those who teach" (AC 1571). That there is strife between Abram's herdsmen and Lot's herdsmen shows a picture of the disagreement between what is "teaching" the internal level of young Jesus and what is "teaching" His external level. The deeper part of Jesus is being taught by celestial love coming from Jehovah, and the external part of Jesus is being taught by what He is sensing outwardly. At this time, the two points of view are not in agreement. Evil influences that come through Jesus' finite maternal heredity are clouding His sensory awareness, tempting Him to false and confused ideas.

Perhaps an example of this occurs as young Jesus is first taught the rituals of worship (see AC 1572). At that time, in the culture in which Jesus was growing up, strict adherence to the outer Jewish rituals took precedence over true inner worship of the heart. These cultural values, even if taught by kind and obedient guardians such as Mary and Joseph, are not compatible with the truth that Jesus' Divine Soul is teaching – that true worship is first a matter of the heart. Later, the adult Jesus will speak about this to the crowds many times. But now the young boy must begin to separate conflicts between His outer learning and His inner learning.

As frequently happens in His development, the boy Jesus is shown a vision. His Soul illuminates how beautiful His external level will be when fully joined with His internal love, Jehovah. This is described when **"Lot lifted up his eyes and saw all the plain of Jordan that it was all well watered. . . ."** Here, Jehovah flows strongly into the boy Jesus' mind, and there is a harmony. At these times the Lord comes into a state of oneness with His Soul (AC 1583). He experiences the sweet uplifting that the future completed state of oneness will bring. The beauty of that state was as **"the garden of Jehovah" (Gen. 13:10).**

"And Jehovah said to Abram after Lot had been separated from him, 'Lift up your eyes now and look from the place where you are, towards the north, and towards the south, and towards the east, and towards the west' " (Gen. 13:14).

At this time the child Jesus is in a state that allows Him, from His Soul, to see things to come. Looking toward the north, south, east, and west means to see all people, as many as there are in the universe (AC 1601). Those Jesus sees in the north are people who are in darkness in regard to spiritual truths and knowledges; those in the south are people who are in spiritual light. Those in the east are people who lived in the past, and also those in celestial love, while those in the west are people who will live in the future (AC 1605). Jehovah gives the boy the ability to see all people who are or will be in heaven: from the past, the present, and the future. What great joy this brings to this Divine boy whose whole longing is to lead people to heaven! He is being shown His prayers fulfilled. The past and future can be seen clearly only by God, and in this case the human essence within the boy Jesus experiences a glimpse of this Divine all-seeing power.

Chapter Three

THE FIRST TEMPTATIONS OF JESUS

THE BATTLE OF THE KINGS
GENESIS 14

- ✦ In the land where Abram lives there is an alliance of four kings and an opposing alliance of five kings.
- ✦ The alliance of the four kings defeats the alliance of the five kings.
- ✦ Chedorlaomer, one of the kings in the four-king alliance, captures Lot, who lives in Sodom.
- ✦ One citizen of Sodom escapes and tells Abram about the capture of Lot.
- ✦ Abram attacks and defeats Chedorlaomer, freeing Lot.
- ✦ Two kings in the land of Canaan meet and thank Abram when he returns from defeating Chedorlaomer.

Once the child Jesus has this vision of the north, south, east and west — of the past and future — it is inevitable that the hells will attack. They hate a love that undermines them, and they especially hate the Lord's love for the salvation of the whole of humankind.

The Lord's vision of His purposes fulfilled is a declaration of war to the devils and satans. But Jesus is only in early childhood. Can the hells attack Him then?

An answer is found in Greek mythology. When attacked by two spotted serpents sent by a jealous Hera, Hercules — then an infant in his cradle — destroyed them with his bare hands. In mythology, Hercules was the strongest man who ever lived. The ancients, those living in the distant past, knew from an Ancient Word that in His earliest childhood the Lord would confront the hells for the first time. That this actually happened is revealed in the internal sense of Genesis 14.

The alliance of four kings (Amraphel, king of Shinar; Arioch, king of Ellasar; Chedorlaomer, king of Elam; and Tidal, king of nations) represents the qualities within the child Jesus from which He will wage His first wars against the hells. **The opposing alliance of five kings (led by the kings of Sodom and Gomorrah)** represents the evil desires and false persuasions (AC 1663) that the Lord will fight against. These are not minor combats. They are crucial to the salvation of the people of this planet.

Temptations are cyclical. They come, go, and return later. The Lord's first temptations occur now, in childhood. They come again on deeper planes. Each time, He conquers, and each time He establishes a more complete union with His Soul. This temptation combat happens with inner agony every time, for the height of His love for others provokes the hells to a vicious depth of attack.

Prior to the war between the four kings and the five, the good kings (under Chedorlaomer) had been victorious in many battles with evil nations. These nations included the most cruel on earth, said to be of a "similar kind to the Nephilim" (AC 1673). The "Nephilim" are symbolic of some of the worst devils in existence, the inhabitants of the lowest hells. Inevitably they attack the Lord as early in His life as possible, for they wish to approach Him when He is most vulnerable, and they are permitted to do so.

Dreadful persuasions filled those tribes who lived before the "flood" (the symbolic end of the Church of those times — the "flood" of false ideas depicted in the Noah story), especially the Nephilim. Their persuasions were dark and poisonous lies.

"Such were the unspeakably horrible nations against whom the Lord fought in earliest childhood, and whom He overcame. And unless the Lord by His coming into the world had overcome them, nobody at all would be alive today on this planet" (AC 1673:2).

When the Lord fights these hells, He still has humanly childish qualities. He fights partially from a sense of merit, or self-credit, as we do in our own earliest temptations (AC 1661:3-5). But this merit is there in innocence and ignorance. In innocence lies the greatest spiritual power. The hells fall back before it.

When He is a child, the Lord's sense of merit is akin to our own; that is, when we believe to be functioning from our own power instead of God's power. At first, the child Jesus is not clearly aware that He is fighting from the power of His Divine Soul. But later, when fully joined to His Soul, Jesus would become Merit itself in a pure and good sense, with no negative connotation. He alone, when glorified, is Good itself. All of our good is from Him.

The four kings prevailed in every battle, including the final great battle against the evil alliance of five kings. These battles of the good alliance represent the temptations that the Lord experiences in childhood, about which nothing is recorded in the New Testament (AC 1690).

What might these trials be like for the child Jesus? Though evil spirits had lurked nearby from the moment He was born, Jehovah did not permit them to attack. Just as with us, Jehovah does not permit temptations, or attacks by the forces of hell, until Jesus first learns something about the distinctions between good and evil. With us, these full assaults do not happen until adulthood. But with

34

this boy, our Savior, they happen in youngest childhood. Once Jesus has gained some initial knowledge and insight, the hells are let loose, and they attack with a vengeance.

The devils that attack the child Jesus are similar to the Nephilim (AC 1673). These spirits especially want to snuff out in their victim all ability to think, to possess the victim's will and understanding, so that the victim feels scarcely alive. Just as Jesus' mind is first opening and learning truth, wicked spirits work to suffocate that new understanding, to negate true ideas, to cry out that "it is not so" and instead insert their poisonous lies. They try with all their might to stop young Jesus from thinking the truth and seeing what is good.

As finite humans, we feel such dire attacks of temptations only as a dull pain. Young Jesus, however, has incredible depth of perceptive awareness from His Divine Soul and His celestial love. He feels these attacks acutely, severely, as sharp and torturous pain. Perhaps He feels these attacks of the hells, both against Himself and also in the events going on around Him in the streets of Nazareth. Perhaps this small boy feels, with acute perception, the intensity of the unkindness and false ideas that the hells are inflicting on others. Because His deepest love is for the happiness of humankind, these perceptions and temptations fill Him with great pain.

But these wicked spirits do not conquer Jesus. Using what good and truth He has gained (the alliance of four kings), though it is not yet pure, the boy faces and resists these intense false persuasions. The alliance of four kings is victorious, though some members of the evil alliance of five kings escape into the mountains, waiting to bring trouble at a later time.

The Lord's intense love for humankind and His desire to save us are demonstrated by His willingness to endure these trials, and the fact that they begin for Him in what for others is the age of innocence and ignorance. He is born with a love for our salvation, and fostering this is to be His inmost joy (AC 2034). This is what sustains Him in childhood.

However, not all of His states are those of temptations or trial. Jesus has delightful times when He is at One with His Father, and in this there is a joy inconceivable to us.

The Old Testament account of the battles representing these earliest temptations says that **Abram's nephew Lot was captured by Chedorlaomer and taken north near Damascus.** Lot represents the Lord's external level, or His sensory awareness (see AC 1698). Chedorlaomer, who symbolizes a sense of merit or self-credit, captures this. Though a battle has been won, the Lord's external level is captured by a sense of having won the battle on His own, without the power of His Divine Soul. Captivity by merit is a limited state and has a strong degree of self-love within it (AC 3993:9-11). Such merit has its place in the beginning of "regeneration" or the lifelong process of being spiritually reborn, but if we are ever to become angels it must eventually be removed. The Lord here shows the way.

In the Lord's case, there is an almost immediate perception by His interior mind (represented by Abram the Hebrew) that the captivity by merit has taken place. The Word says that **"one who had escaped came and told it to Abram the Hebrew" (Gen.14: 13).** The "one who had escaped" is a perception by the child Jesus—a perception from an inner plane of goodness—that it is wrong to be captivated by merit. As a child He sees this, and He wishes to free Himself from this entrapment (AC 1702, 1707:5).

Feeling merit is a potent enchantment, but it has its uses. We need it to get us through many states and many spiritual battles. This is especially true in infancy and childhood, when a sense of merit or self-credit is appropriate and needed (see AC 1667:2). With such merit, "The ignorance excuses, and the innocence makes it appear good" (*Ibid.*) Children hunger for appropriate praise; it will lead them later to praise of the Lord (see AC 1661).

Recognition of merit's usefulness is a key element behind the "self-esteem" movement that is popular today. But when the Lord feels merit, He eventually puts it aside. The time comes when we must also put aside childish things. Otherwise we will be captivated by merit and carried away into the north, into the deep obscurity of spiritual night. However, when merit is recognized as narcissistic and is rejected, the Lord walks into our hearts. He shares His own experience with us.

Abram fought against Chedorlaomer and his allies at night, conquering them with only 318 trained warriors. It was, it seems, a surprise attack, and the victory was complete. **They liberated Lot and his family and belongings and allowed them to be returned to the land of Canaan.** This is a triumph. Lot, that is, the Lord's external awareness, is freed from all sense of merit. This brings an influx of joy to the child. His very Soul comes down to bless Him. These victories of the Lord in His first temptations are crucial to His whole life on earth, to His future of becoming One with His Soul.

When Abram and Lot returned to the land of Canaan, they were greeted by a number of kings. But one person there, a mysterious figure, seems to come out of nowhere.

"And Melchizedek, king of Salem, brought out bread and wine, and he was priest to God most high. And he blessed Abram" **(Gen. 14:18-19).**

Melchizedek represents the celestial level within the Lord. The Divine blesses the child after this stunning victory (AC 1725), and the bread and wine given to Abram prefigure the Holy Supper. The Lord gains Divine "remains" in these earliest victories (AC 1734), and in the victories does not use or retain any of the methods or tactics or motivations of the hells (AC 1739-1748), as when Abram says to the King of Sodom "**. . .nor anything that is yours**

will I take" (Gen. 14:23). It is the same with His invitation to us: if we turn to Him in dire temptation, He will lead us to victory and freedom.

Chapter Four

COMFORT AND INSIGHTS FOR THE CHILD JESUS

THE VISION OF THE STARS
GENESIS 15

> ✛ Jehovah comes to Abram in a vision and makes a promise to him that his descendants will be in number like the stars in the sky.

"After these events, the word of Jehovah came to Abram in a vision, saying, 'Fear not, Abram, I am a shield to you, your exceeding great reward' " (Gen. 15:1).

The Lord in earliest childhood has just experienced His first temptations, and they have involved strong love and powerful despair. The conflicts are "directed against the love He cherished toward the entire human race" (AC 1778). Jehovah then inflows into the child Jesus with comfort: **"Fear not, Abram, I am a shield to you" (Gen. 15:1).** This comfort comes "in a vision," a vision which brings an "inmost revelation" (AC 1784).

After these events the child Jesus laments that there is no spiritual depth in the church on earth. This is embodied in Abram's words **"seeing I go childless" (Gen. 15:2).** Jesus can only see a church of an external nature without inner heart. Would this be His heir? Would there be no real celestial love, no mutual love and heavenly kindness? He can see that "there was no internal dimension to the church" (AC 1797).

Jehovah then re-assures Jesus, promising that there will be an heir or future church with people in celestial love and love of the neighbor (AC 1800). A living church will be reborn on earth. Jesus (or Abram, His representative) is shown this in a vivid way.

Picture the Lord as a young boy, perhaps younger than twelve, going out at night beyond the outskirts of Nazareth in Galilee. His Soul leads Him to look up at the stars. The atmosphere is crystal clear, and the young child sees myriads of stars. His Soul then gives Him, as he gazes upward, a "mental view of the universe."

We now know that one galaxy holds millions of stars. And though it seems incredible, there are millions of galaxies. Jesus also sees, through the correspondence of these stars, the billions of people who have become angels in the universe, for each star symbolizes a society of angels. Jehovah says to Jesus in internal conversation, "See all these millions of stars. That is how many angels, past, present and future, there are and will be" (see AC 1805, 1810).

Learning from "correspondences" is a way of using the relationship of all things of heaven with all things on earth. This method of seeing — of using physical things to learn about spiritual things — is a whole method or paradigm of insight. It is not an entirely new paradigm, for it was known to the Most Ancient people and to the people of the Ancient Church as well. But it has long since been forgotten. Jehovah uses correspondences here in teaching Jesus.

The two worlds, natural and spiritual, marvelously co-respond to each other. The people of the Most Ancient Church on earth knew instinctively that our earthly sun corresponds to the Sun in heaven, or to the Lord's Love. They instinctively knew the correspondences of mountains, seas, lakes, meadows, woods, flowers, animals, birds, and, in fact, all things of creation.

A touch of this instinctive feeling or perception is left with us today, perhaps from our remains or from the very order of our souls. We see a soaring snowcapped mountain and sense its power. We do not know without instruction that high mountains correspond to love of the Lord, a love soaring to the skies, yet we seem to feel something of this. We sense that the outer heights of nature symbolize inner heights of the mind and heart. So also when we see sparkling waters on an ocean or lake, delight touches us and we feel their beauty. We do not know without instruction that such waters correspond to living truths, but nevertheless we feel a delight. And so it is with gardens, woods, graceful animals, and many other things of nature.

The Writings of Emanuel Swedenborg reveal a myriad of correspondences, and knowing correspondences can greatly enhance the effect that nature has on our minds and hearts. From this new knowledge given to Swedenborg, it can be more than an occasional instinctive feeling; it can again become the "knowledge of knowledges" (NJHD 261, AC 1806, 1807).

What the Lord sees that night, when Jehovah brings Him (represented by Abram) outside, and says, **"Look now towards heaven and count the stars, if you are able to count them" (Gen. 15:5)** stands as a prophecy for this new knowledge being used in a New Church on earth. Jesus is inspired and encouraged by this vision.

When the boy Jesus sees this vision, He knows that the countless stars represent all the good in heaven and on earth. After His first temptations, this reassurance means much to Him. Abram **"believed in Jehovah, and Jehovah reckoned it to him as righteousness" (Gen. 15:6).**

"What is meant here by "believing in Jehovah" is that the Lord was filled repeatedly with an inmost confidence and faith. He was shown, and He believed, that because it was pure love from which He was fighting for the salvation of the whole human race, He

41

could not be anything but victorious" (AC 1812).

The Lord offers this same hope for us in our temptations. His pure love, glorified, conquers death, and rises in resurrection. Because of this, when our bodies die, His Divine love also lifts us up. No force can resist this.

Chapter Five

THE FIRST RATIONAL OF THE LORD AS A CHILD

ISHMAEL
GENESIS 16

✦ Sarai, Abram's wife, is unable to have a child, so she has her servant Hagar conceive a child from Abram.

✦ Hagar gives birth to a son named Ishmael.

✦ Hagar now feels superior to her mistress. Sarai is disturbed by this, and tries to humble her. Hagar runs away.

✦ An angel appears to Hagar and tells her to return to Sarai. The angel also tells her that Ishmael will be a wild man, struggling against everyone.

Ishmael represents the first "rational," or first reasoning ability, of the Lord and of ourselves. Understanding the nature of this first reasoning ability is not a minor issue. For if Ishmael is allowed to be the primary heir, if he is allowed to rule unchallenged, then spiritually our civilization will perish. Ishmael the mocker would supplant the future Isaac, the future son of Abram and Sarai, who symbolizes true or spiritual thinking. Humanity begins in the inmost of this true rational, which is the "Isaac" reasoning ability, not the "Ishmael" (AC 2194).

Who is Ishmael spiritually? What is his role? The drama in the

Genesis story (chapter 16) gives the key. **Since Sarai was barren, it was necessary that Ishmael be born to provide an heir at this time.** Since the Lord wishes to walk the pathway of human development, Ishmael, the temporary heir, must be born to Him also. He too, before achieving a spiritual rationality, comes into this first rational. How the Lord handles this lower-level rational is a key to the future establishment of a New Church on this earth.

Jesus is aware of a deep lack within Himself (AC 1892). The child does not yet have a true or Divine rational level of His mind. He feels this barrenness and yearns for a true inner level of thinking.

Jesus yearns to understand the Divine purpose and nature of creation fully and deeply. He wishes for this, not for His own sake, but because He knows this capability is needed to save us. To save humankind is His love, His life. But Sarai, who symbolizes pure and heavenly truth allied to the goodness in Him, was barren. The pure truth deep within young Jesus was not yet able to produce a rational way of thinking. Spiritually rational thinking is the intermediary that can join heavenly and worldly knowledge.

When Sarai saw she was barren, she went to Abram and said: "See now, Jehovah has restrained me from bearing children. Please, go in to my maid; perhaps I shall obtain children by her" (Gen. 16:2). "So Hagar bore Abram a son; and Abram named his son. . .Ishmael" (Gen. 16:15). Deep within Him, Jesus perceives that He cannot produce a reasoning ability straight from His love of pure, heavenly truth (Sarai). There must be an outer basis. A love for external knowledge, learned from the world around Him, must be joined to His Divine Internal (Abram). Hagar, who is brought to Abram by Sarai herself, represents this love for external knowledge, and it is from this that the Lord's first rational thinking is born. This is an outer reasoning, thinking from worldly knowledge.

When is this "Ishmael rational" born within Him? I believe He is younger than twelve years old. The second or Isaac rational seems to be speaking in the temple when the Lord is twelve. For all who heard Jesus then "were astonished at His understanding and answers" (Luke 2:47). And He said to Joseph and Mary, "Did you not know that I must be about My Father's business?" or literally, "in my Father's things?" (Luke 2:49).

If there had been no hereditary evil in the human race, the Divine rational would, at the right time, have been born immediately with the Lord. Sarai would not have been barren. But the Lord took on hereditary evil tendencies with His birth from Mary. He did this deliberately so that He might experience our pathway and out of love show us the way.

That a love of worldly knowledge (Hagar) is the mother of Ishmael fits his representation exactly. This initial ability to reason, the "first rational," is only from a natural level. It comes from a marriage of an internal love with strong outer curiosity. The first rational is necessary for mental progress, because the ability to reason is the first step toward deeper thinking, and toward finally seeing spiritual truths.

Unfortunately for us, we have hereditary evil tendencies. With us, these tendencies bring conceit to this reasoning ability. That is why the name "Ishmael" has a pejorative ring to it. As the Word puts it, Ishmael **"will be a wild-ass man; his hand will be against all, and the hand of all against him; and he will dwell in opposition to all his brothers" (Gen. 17:12).**

This first rational in us typically first appears as childhood is ending and young adulthood beginning. What is a person like in this state?

"He is quick to find fault, makes no allowances, is against all, regards everyone as being in error, is instantly prepared to rebuke, to chasten, and to punish, shows no pity, does not apply himself and makes no effort to redirect people's thinking; for he views everything from the standpoint of truth, and nothing from the standpoint of good. In short, he is a hard person" (AC 1949:2).

An even lower element in this first reasoning is seen when it does not acknowledge truth, but rather reasons from the senses alone and is negative to all spiritual truth.

What might this "Ishmael rational" look like in the young Jesus? Once He is actively and eagerly gaining knowledge from the world around Him and forming His first rational conclusions, Jesus feels the stirring of disturbing tendencies in His finite human heredity. From this maternal heredity arise inclinations to judge and criticize, to make conclusions based on outer evidence alone, and to scoff at deep, inner truth. **In Genesis, this scoffing is first represented by the fact that Hagar "despised" her barren mistress once she found herself pregnant.** This first rational state (AC 1911) lacks respect for deep, inner truth that can't be "proved" by outer evidence.

From His deep, inner love of spiritual truth (Sarai) Jesus is greatly upset by the arrogance attached to this first rational level (pregnant Hagar). **In Genesis, Sarai complains to Abram of Hagar's behavior, and Abram gives her permission to deal with her handmaid in any way she sees fit. And so "Sarai deals harshly with Hagar," or in other words "humbles her."**

Jesus' internal level (Abram) enables Him, from His deep love of heavenly truth (Sarai), to subjugate this outer reasoning ability and to work to drive out the negative attitudes and lack of respect that attach themselves to it. This involves much conflict within the young Jesus, and so it is said that Sarai deals harshly with Hagar.

At first, this first rational level in Jesus does not want to be subjugated, and so it is said that **Hagar runs away from her mistress, Sarai. But then, in the wilderness, the Angel of Jehovah comes to Hagar, and speaks to her. The Angel tells Hagar to go back and submit to her mistress, and then describes the nature of the son that will be born to her. As Hagar listens, she softens, and**

marvels at the power of the "God Who Sees."

The voice of Jehovah, represented by the Angel, comes down into the first rational stirrings within the mind of young Jesus. His Divine Soul enlightens Jesus as to what this first reasoning ability will be like if it does not submit to the guidance of inner truth, which holds the things of God and heavenly love above the things of the world. If this first rational does submit to higher truth, then it will multiply and grow, learning more and more wonders from the natural world which reflect the glory of its Creator. **The Angel promises Hagar that if she respects and obeys her mistress, God will multiply her descendants exceedingly (Gen. 16:10).**

Jesus marvels at the wisdom of this, and willingly allows this new rational level to be subjugated and cleansed by His deep love of spiritual truth. **Hagar obediently returns to her mistress.**

Every mentally sound child or youth comes into the use of reason. This gift can either turn us away from the Lord or open us up to Him with new breadth. When it is said that the human, the true human, begins in the "inmost of the rational" (AC 2194), it means that the highest part of our intelligence is to think, to understand, and to comprehend things above our senses. If we see from a heavenly love, then the rational becomes fully alive to the beauty of the Lord and of creation. The Writings of Swedenborg speak to this highest level of the human mind — to the rational that sees from kindness or love.

Ishmael was to be cast out, and Isaac was to take his place. Therefore the first rational is to be expelled, and the second or spiritual rational is to take its place (AC 1949:2, 1950). The cynical qualities and the hard nature of the first reasoning ability must be shunned and removed before we can be truly human. The one thing that softens the hardness of that initial way of thinking is goodness — the good of kindness. This is the heart of the second rational.

The Lord as a boy thinks from higher truth and from higher love, and from these He subdues the evil tendencies that affect His first reasoning. Because He does this, He makes it possible for us to do the same. With the Lord's help we are able to fight against false reason — reason that is tied to conceit. Our minds can become free to see and love Divine truth. "If you abide in My Word, then you are My disciples indeed, and you shall know the truth, and the truth shall make you free" (John 8:31,32). The Lord as a boy paves the way for us. In the temple at age twelve, He shows the results of this: "All who heard Him were astonished at His understanding and answers" (Luke 2:47).

At every step of His growth and glorification, the Lord reveals Divine principles. His first perception as an infant, that we are to ascend from lower things to higher ones, is the key to life. We are here on earth to ascend to heaven. In overcoming the cruel, persuasive, and controlling spirits called the Nephilim in His first temptations, He shows the path of rebirth for us and helps to clear the way. In viewing the stars He not only sees the future angelic heaven, but also shows a new way of thinking, by which we can use external things to see spiritual or internal things.

In His subduing of the first rational, the Lord indicates the path to true thinking, and to being truly human. If we reason from outer evidence alone, received through our senses, we will never believe. This first rational thinking is Ishmael, and it is a rebel. But if love or kindness comes to us, the Lord opens our eyes, just as His eyes open from love in order to see the Ishmael rational for what it is. If we are willing to acknowledge a hard truth — that it is conceit that blinds our eyes — and then shun that arrogance and pray for the Lord's enlightenment, we will "perceive what is true" from the Lord's influx and light (see AC 6047).

The negative principle, thinking from the senses and from conceit, has viciously attacked churches in the past. It also destroys our own individual perception or sight of truth. Our arrogance does not like to admit this, true though it is.

But the affirmative principle, thinking from the Lord's light, opens our eyes (*Ibid.*). This is a promise to each of us, and it is true. In the journey and development of the Lord as a boy, Isaac replaces Ishmael.

Chapter Six

THE SALVATION OF HUMANKIND

A COVENANT
GENESIS 17

> ✦ **Jehovah makes a covenant with Abram, that he will be a father of many nations, and Jehovah changes his name to Abraham.**

> ✦ **The sign of the covenant between Jehovah and Abraham, as well as his descendants, is that Abraham and his descendants will be circumcised.**

> ✦ **Abraham, Ishmael and all the men of his house are circumcised.**

Jehovah is Love itself. He, in essence, is the deepest possible love for others, the desire to be one with them, and to make them happy from Himself (see TCR 43). Jesus as a boy was not yet One with Jehovah. But He, too, was moved by deep love — a love for the saving of each of us. It is easy to use the term "love." But Jesus' love is so tender, so gentle, that it is only in our own most sensitive moments that we can perceive something of His nature (AC 2077:1,2).

In Genesis 17 **Jehovah makes a covenant with Abram**. This covenant pledges a closer union of Jehovah and the human part or human essence of Jesus. Jesus the boy is growing up. "He increased in wisdom and stature and in favor with God and men" (Luke 2:52). He has reasoning ability, represented by Ishmael. He has subordinated His reasoning to the higher love within Him, bringing in Isaac as the future new heir. This brings Jesus closer to His Soul, Jehovah, and leads to the covenant spoken of in this chapter.

A special event now happens. **Jehovah said to Abram, "no longer will your name be called Abram, but your name will be Abraham, for I have made you the father of a multitude of nations" (Gen. 17:5).** This means that Jesus "will cast off the [finite] human" and that "He will put on the Divine" (AC 2008). This does not happen instantaneously. It is accomplished step by step (AC 2010). The letter "h" was here added to Abram's name. This letter represents what is Divine, and therefore what is gently yet powerfully loving. Sarai also had "h" added to her name, with similar meaning.

The Lord as an infant, child, and youth is the most loving and caring person ever present on this earth. Now, in becoming nearer to the Divine itself, He becomes even more loving. This does not mean that we lose Him. He becomes closer to us, more compassionate, and finally Divinely loving. This is vital. By becoming Divine even in His Human, He puts on powers and qualities no mortal person has. He has the power to make His love for us truly effective. He is with us now, where we live, love, think and feel. He lifts us up from death. He lifts us up, if we are willing, from inner spiritual death. He cannot do this effectively in His human essence before He becomes Divine. This addition of the letter "h" to Abram's name is cause for joy.

Because the Lord was born on earth, where He "glorified" or made Divine His rational, His natural, His sensuous, and His very body, He becomes present with us in a way never before possible. He becomes present to save us.

The sign of the covenant between Jehovah and Abraham

was circumcision (Gen. 17:10). It was also a covenant between Abraham and his "seed" or descendants. Spiritually this covenant is between the Lord and all people, and it leads to each person's rebirth, for all that are willing. Circumcision symbolizes "the removal and rejection of those things that were impeding and defiling celestial love" (AC 2039). To reject, from the Lord's power, those lusts and evils that impede our deepest love is to circumcise the heart.

Jehovah's covenant with Abraham led to the further covenant with us. As we circumcise our hearts with deep prayer to the Lord, He inflows into us with the three most vital loves in creation: conjugial love, the love of infants, and mutual love or love for society (*Ibid.*). The term "conjugial love" is one that Swedenborg uses to describe a love between married partners that is spiritual and heavenly in quality. Conjugial is the principal of all good loves. Within it are the highest uses and most tender receptions of the Lord. In its essence, conjugial love is love of the Lord received. A husband and wife who look in innocence to the Lord receive conjugial love, and from this flows their love of infants and love of their children's innocence.

What is more beautiful to see than the love between a devoted husband and wife? This love comes as a result of the union between the Lord's Divine, the part that is Jehovah, and the Human, the part that came on earth as Jesus. The Lord's inmost joy was to foresee that out of the union of the Divine and Human in Himself would come individual rebirths in many, many human hearts, including the future reception of true marriage love (AC 2034, 2039).

Chapter Seven

"His Mercy Is Forever"

Isaac's Birth Foretold
Genesis 18

- ✦ Jehovah appears to Abraham as three men (angels), and Abraham and Sarah feed them.
- ✦ Jehovah tells Abraham that he and Sarah will have a child.
- ✦ When the angels are going to leave, Abraham looks toward Sodom with them, and discusses with Jehovah His plan to destroy Sodom.
- ✦ Abraham begs Jehovah to spare the city.

In these days in Nazareth the boy Jesus is open to learning from His Soul. This openness is represented first by Jehovah and His three angels' visiting Abraham in Mamre; second, by Jehovah's message to Abraham and Sarah about Isaac's future conception and birth; and finally by Jehovah's and Abraham's looking down upon Sodom and Gomorrah, and Abraham's pleading with Jehovah that they be spared. These three events describe Jesus' learning about the perfect Oneness in God, the coming birth of His Divine rational level, and about the extent of Jehovah's mercy.

"And Jehovah appeared to Abraham in the oak-groves of Mamre, and he was sitting in the tent door, as the day was getting warmer" (Gen. 18:1). By "the day getting warmer" is meant symbolically that unselfish love is becoming stronger in Jesus. From this increasing love He is open to learning. **"And he lifted up his eyes and saw, and behold, three men standing over him. And he saw, and ran from the tent door to meet them, and bowed towards the ground" (Gen. 18:2).** Jesus, like Abraham's vision many years earlier, sees three angels standing before Him, and He realizes these three represent the trinity in God.

He recognizes that He will now learn from His Soul more about the One God — about God's unity and the trinity within Him. He feels humbled by this instruction, but also feels great joy. He loves to learn these things, especially from His Soul Who He knows is Love itself.

Think of the distance, the immeasurable difference, between God and a finite human being. God is Infinite Divine Love itself. We are finite, yet still human in His image. Jesus at this time has a comparable separation between Himself and His Divine Soul as far as His human essence is concerned.

As Abraham is speaking here, he represents the Lord as to His "human before it was made Divine" (AC 2154). This is comparable to our separation from God, but with the Lord as a boy there are marked differences. He is born with a love for saving others. His Soul is Divine – God. Nevertheless, as to His human essence at this point, He is still finite.

Now Jehovah has drawn near, appearing to Jesus in a vision. The boy is deeply moved, and desires that Jehovah stay and teach Him, and be close to Him. **Abraham**, representing the boy Jesus, **asked the angels or Jehovah to stay and refresh themselves, and said that He would prepare food and drink for them (Gen. 18:4-8).**

This symbolizes how the Divine accommodates itself to communicate with the child. And the boy Jesus also comes into a special state so that He can directly communicate with His Soul. You feel the strong wishes of the two to reach to communicate with each other. The Divine draws nearer to the boy by putting on something natural, and the boy draws nearer to His Soul by putting on something celestial (AC 2137).

There is a rich and full communication. The Word says that **"Abraham stood before the angels [or Jehovah] under the tree, and they ate" (Gen. 18:8).** The key words "and they ate" signify this communication of Jehovah and the boy. This brings Jesus special happiness (AC 2147), because He is taught clearly how His purpose on earth may be fulfilled. He is further taught how He will become One with His Soul, and how this union will lead to the Holy Spirit being sent out from Him. This is the trinity in One Person. By this union, when He has become the Divine Human, He will proceed to redeem and save countless human beings, and hopefully each one of us.

When this first instruction is completed, Jehovah turns to the second phase of the child's instruction. This instruction is about the conception and birth of Isaac, or the Divine rational, and that His rational was to "cast off the human and be made Divine" (AC 2138). This step is vital to His goals. Without a glorified rational, the Lord would lack the means to save humankind. The Ishmael within Him cannot do this. He sees His own present inadequacies, His strong need for a true rational or ability to reason from a heavenly perspective, and He wishes intensely for its birth.

Jehovah told Abraham that Sarah his wife would bear a son in about a year's time. Sarah overheard this promise and laughed in disbelief. She thought that she and Abraham were far too old to have a child. Her disbelief illustrates our own lack of trust in the Lord's inner miracles.

In our lower states we find it incredible that something higher and more beautiful can be born within us. The birth of the Lord in the human heart seems unbelievable at times. The coming of living faith to us as adults seems incredible. To this the Lord our Creator and Father says, **"Will anything be too wonderful for Jehovah?" (Gen. 18:14).** Don't we experience miracles? Don't we fall in love? Isn't faith born in our hearts?

One part of Jesus cannot believe the Divine rational will be born in Him. Here, Sarah represents "merely human rational truth present within the Lord" (AC 2139). This merely human rational truth laughs at Divine truth, for Divine truth is beyond its comprehension (AC 2139). His Soul then reveals to Jesus the fact that despite the limitations of His finite human heredity, a Divine rational *will* soon be born within Him.

In the history of the human race this birth of the Divine rational with the boy Jesus has startling meaning, for it brings the Divine Human into reality on the plane of His rational level. From this glorified rational, from that time until eternity, comes the salvation of each person. Within the child there is recognition of this, and surpassing joy and gratitude, *for this birth was to change the world.*

It is true that further development is needed to make this Divine birth complete, but the miracle is about to take place.

The third phase of Jesus' being taught by Jehovah is now to begin. It concerns the nature of good and evil within humankind. **Jehovah's and Abraham's going to the plateau edge and looking down on Sodom and Gomorrah** represents a viewing of the state of the human race. These cities had fallen into terrible perversions, and now an examination of their states was about to take place, and judgment if necessary. **Abraham pleaded with Jehovah to spare Sodom and Gomorrah from destruction. He begged Jehovah to spare them if there were fifty good people there, then if there were forty-five, then if there were fewer and fewer, even down to ten.** Abraham's pleading represents Jesus' great love and concern for humankind, and His fear that no one could be saved. For

Jehovah showed Abraham "the face of Sodom" (Gen. 18:16), which represents the evil within human hearts.

At times we tend to look upon evil simplistically. We know it is destructive, a terribly negative force; yet we often fail to see the full cruelty and hate within it. Jesus is about to see this, with Jehovah His Soul at His side. Upon viewing it, "He wished to depart from that perception" (AC 2222). He is born with a love for our salvation. His very heart, His very nature, is to love each human being. Now He is seeing the depth of evil in humankind. The effect of seeing this is direct: He is "struck with horror" (*Ibid.*). He wishes to withdraw from the vision.

Yet this child is born to be our Savior. To fulfill His mission, the Lord on earth has to know fully both the evil and good states of human beings. For the sake of fulfilling His love, He has to know the truth. Then He knows how to help each of us. He must confront a reality that He at first does not wish to face. But He does face it, out of His love. At the same time, as a boy, He has only a limited perception of the mercy of His Soul, of Jehovah. He doesn't really know how His Soul, which He feels then as separate from Himself, will react to this awful sight of evil.

Jesus cannot bear to have His love utterly defeated by human evil; He cares too much, loves too deeply. But what if this is the only possibility? In His present state of development He does not know that His Soul, Jehovah, is mercy itself. In His still ignorant and limited but compassionate Human, He begs Jehovah to save as many as possible. He tries to "intercede" for humankind, unaware that Jehovah always judges from goodness and works to bring into heaven all that are willing to respond.

The boy Jesus, with Jehovah, now views the various states of humankind throughout the earth, from the most regenerate, or spiritually developed, to the least regenerate, and then to those confirmed in evil. The descending numbers for which Jesus pleads with Jehovah to spare the human race (fifty, forty-five, forty, thirty, twenty, and ten) represent lesser and lesser degrees of good within various people on earth. By means of this looking at humankind together with His Soul, the boy Jesus is to learn many beautiful things, and He has the chance for His human love to be strengthened in a tender way.

Abraham first pleaded with Jehovah to spare Sodom if there were only fifty good people there. The number "fifty" represents those people on earth who have in their hearts true ideas filled with goodness (AC 2261). Jehovah said, yes, Sodom (or humankind) would be spared, or saved, for the sake of such innocent good people.

Humankind is also spared if there are those who have less good than those represented by "fifty," but whose goodness is joined with truth. These are the "forty-five" (AC 2269). Those who are victorious in temptations, greater or lesser, are also causes for humankind's salvation — "forty" and "thirty" (AC 2272-3, AC 2276).

The Lord's entire goal is the salvation both of individuals and of human life on this planet as a whole. Therefore this planet will be spared for the sake of children and their salvation, and for the sake of Gentiles who walk in innocence, surely many millions of people (represented by "twenty").

How gentle Jehovah's mercy is! And this is to become the mercy of Jesus Christ as He becomes One with His Soul. In his final plea, Abraham asks that Sodom be spared for the sake of ten good people. The number "ten" represents the qualities of innocence and goodness that remain from childhood. If there are those who have not destroyed these innocent "remains" through confirmed choices of evil, then they too will be elevated into heaven.

Every decent human being is at times depressed over his or her evil. We feel then that there is nothing good enough within us to ever achieve heaven. This type of humility is not bad for us if we don't then give in to evil. Instead, we may think about the sparing of Sodom for only "ten," and pray to the Lord for His presence and help. His mercy is infinite and deeply loving. What He is saying here to each of us is, "I love you, and will save you, if you are only willing." We need only to respond from the heart and show this by obeying His commandments, for this preserves our hidden innocence.

Jehovah's power to save is astounding and far beyond any finite, human mercy. Jesus learns this on that spiritual plateau overlooking the whole realm of human life, just as Abraham looked down from the Judean plateau upon the Salt Sea valley. To Jesus it is deeply moving and fulfilling of His love for human beings. When Jehovah or the three angels then leave Him, Jesus is in a state of inmost joy. He sees that many, many will be saved, and that His purposes on earth will be fulfilled.

LOT SAVED
Genesis 19

+ **The story shifts to Lot, Abraham's nephew, who lives in the city of Sodom.**

+ **Two angels visit Lot in his home, and the home is attacked by the people of Sodom.**

+ **Lot and his family flee; Sodom and Gomorrah are destroyed.**

Chapter 19 of Genesis tells of the visit of two angels to Lot in Sodom, to lead him and his immediate family out of the city. Judgment was coming upon this depraved city, but first, any good people were to flee to the mountain for safety.

In the Divine drama of the Lord's boyhood on earth, this is a prophecy of a fulfillment of His love for the salvation of humankind. In the rescuing of Lot and his daughters from Sodom, Jesus sees the present and future salvation of uncounted millions of human beings. He is moved at heart, but at the same time He sees the inevitable reality that evil (Sodom) rushes to its own self-judgment. He also realizes that some people will turn back from good and truth, and profane them, just as Lot's wife turned back to look at Sodom and turned into a pillar of salt. He wishes it were not so. He strongly desires the salvation of all, but He sees more and more clearly that there must be spiritual freedom if people are to be human and responsive.

The primary theme of this chapter is rescue and salvation. It is realistic and vital that evil and good be separated in order to protect what is good. But the Lord always reaches out to rescue *any* willing person. Lot was freed. We may be freed. Jesus learns more here about the nature of Divine compassion, and reaches up in His heart towards it.

Chapter Eight

THE ORIGIN OF DOCTRINE

ABRAHAM, SARAH, AND ABIMELECH
GENESIS 20

+ The story shifts back to Abraham and Sarah, who travel south to Gerar.

+ Abraham tells Abimelech, the king of Gerar, that Sarah is his sister, for fear that Abimelech will kill him to take Sarah for his own.

+ God warns Abimelech in a dream not to take Sarah for a wife, so Abimelech restores Sarah to Abraham.

A final preparation is needed before Isaac, or the Divine rational, can be born. **Abraham's and Sarah's sojourning in Gerar of Philistia, and Abraham's calling Sarah his sister** represent this preparation. **Sarah was beautiful, and Abimelech, the king of Gerar, took her to be his future wife. After being warned by God in a dream, he restored Sarah to Abraham and gave him many gifts.**

Hidden in this story is a Divine warning. Also hidden here is how the Lord, as He neared the end of childhood, prepared to receive the Divine "doctrine" or religious principles to live by. In infancy in Egypt, Jesus had been instructed in knowledges and had received insights. Now, in a far more advanced state, He is taught doctrinal things (AC 2496). He is taught how to convert these knowledges and insights into spiritual principles for living.

In His learning, the Lord has a special gift or talent. He is able to be instructed "by continual revelations, and thus by Divine perceptions and thoughts from. . .the Divine. . . .This way of growing wise is not possible with any person, for it flowed in from the Divine itself" (AC 2500:2). This is a method of Divinely perceptive learning that the child Jesus alone has.

When Abraham told Abimilech that Sarah was his sister, he opened the way for a terrible adultery. Abimelech represents principles of faith that are being searched out by sensual reasoning (AC 2510), and his taking Sarah to his house represents the love of using sense-based reasoning to find spiritual truth. This seems like an innocuous thing to do, but it is spiritual adultery and has caused the downfall of every major church on earth and of many reasoning human beings.

We accept into our lives only truth that is gained from a genuinely kind and loving perspective, not from a calculating "prove it to me" attitude. All truth in our lives can be seen only from spiritual love. Love opens the eyes. Sarah representing such truth is a wife. She is not a sister to be taken in adultery by Abimelech (AC 2510, 2568:4, 6047).

Jesus as a boy encounters the problem of reasoning from the senses about matters of faith, because He has this tendency from His heredity through Mary. In His higher thought He sees clearly that such thinking undermines genuine doctrine, and that in the last analysis this approach to the Word springs from conceit. He also sees that this conceit has to be put off, along with the rest of His finite human heredity (AC 2511).

This story of Abraham, Sarah, and Abimelech seems to be an historical case of unintentional adultery. Spiritually, though, for the Lord and for us, it reveals a crucial axiom about external reasoning and its place in the search for faith. This axiom is not in harmony with the attitude prevailing in much of higher education, which believes that "Of course you use reason in determining what is (spiritually) true! The scientific or inductive method is the key to final philosophical truths." It is this ruling principle, termed "the negative principle" in the Writings of Swedenborg, which underlies so much of the thinking in today's world! However, we see a shift away from this type of thinking in many areas, for example in the interest in Eastern thought. The inadequacy of human reason is more and more clearly recognized.

That the Lord confronts this issue in His glorification is a vital reality, because it paves the way for the future release of civilization from lower thinking, from a darkened perception. It enables heavenly light and heavenly love to penetrate the thinking mind. The *human* begins in the *inmost* of the rational mind, and this "inmost" is heavenly love.

Concerning the inverted method of thinking that the Lord considered from His finite maternal human (using reason to establish faith), we read that "He reproved Himself from zeal. . .and here that He felt horror" (AC 2548). What leads Him into thinking of a wrong approach to truth is His finite maternal heredity, and perhaps much more potently, the concern He feels for our limitations and for us. He has to resist reasoning from His limited, outer view of the state of the human race, and instead reason from what He is learning from the perspective of His Divine Soul. By considering the former wrong approach to truth, Jesus learns a great deal, and the "horror" He comes to feel about this inverted approach, symbolized by Abimelech's horror at what he had done, stands as a warning signal to us.

Heavenly loves and truths are potentially present on the higher levels of our minds. Truths can be revealed or disclosed to our higher rational. But our lower rational or reasoning simply <u>does not have</u> the *ability* to see or believe truths and goods that are on a higher or heavenly level. They are above its range of competence. A camel cannot go through the eye of a needle.

Revealed truth may be clearly seen and perceived by our "Isaac" or spiritual rational. That is why the birth of Isaac is so important both in human development and in the Lord's work of becoming One with His Soul. To approach spiritual truth with humility and with the affection of truth is to invite the Lord to open our eyes (AC 6047). A quiet miracle happens. "One thing I know: that whereas I was blind, now I see" (John 9:25).

Chapter Nine

THE BIRTH OF THE DIVINE RATIONAL

ISAAC

GENESIS 21

+ Isaac is born to Abraham and Sarah.

+ Ishmael mocks Isaac during the feast to celebrate Isaac's weaning, so Sarah banishes Hagar and Ishmael.

+ Hagar and Ishmael wander in the wilderness of Beersheba and nearly die of thirst until God leads them to water.

+ Hagar and Ishmael survive and settle in Egypt.

"And Jehovah visited Sarah, as He had said; and Jehovah did unto Sarah as He had spoken. And Sarah conceived and bare Abraham a son in his old age, at the appointed time, as God had spoken with him. And Abraham called the name of his son that was born unto him, whom Sarah bare to him, Isaac" (Gen. 21:3).

In the inmost meaning of this event from Genesis is the culmination of the Lord's entire childhood. What Isaac's birth symbolizes and what it means to humankind is profoundly significant.

With Jesus Christ, when His Divine rational is born, the Divine Human has its beginning.

At this time, the Lord's Divine rational is born from the marriage of good and truth, of the celestial and spiritual, of Abraham and Sarah. From this marriage of good and truth within the Lord comes the potential of the marriage of good and truth *within us.* From this inner marriage comes "all conjugial love" (AC 2618). A truly happy marriage, an eternal marriage, comes only with conjugial love. The hope of receiving this gift is one of the highest hopes in human life. For us then, this birth of Isaac heralds a possible return to innocence, for this can come about only in conjugial love, or the effort toward this love.

Isaac was born, but he was only a tiny infant. He had to be circumcised, grow up, marry, and become established as an adult in his own right. It is the same for the Divine rationality of the Lord. But this development happens quickly with Jesus. With His Divine Soul and special endowments, He comes to the birth of the Divine rational at an early age.

With us, the birth of spiritual rationality is one of the miracles of life. We may have searched on and on for truth, and sometimes any real vision of truth may seem utterly impossible. Finally we can look within ourselves and realize that we have evils that must be put aside before we can ever truly see. We shun evils, especially conceit, and ask the Lord's help. But still we don't see. Then quietly, from we don't know where, comes the *perception*, the seeing, that revealed truth (truth given to humanity by God) *is true* (AC 6047)! This opens up a vista stretching to eternity. It opens up even the hope and promise of future conjugial love.

In the birth of the Divine rational with the Lord, there comes a world of wonder and delight beyond our easy ken. With this birth, the Lord sees the means (the truths) to fulfill His inmost loves. This gives a new character to His human essence. He knows this ability is only in its infancy, but as it grows and is further made Divine, it is part of the means of rescuing us. His heart is deeply moved.

The name "Isaac" is derived from a word meaning "laughter." AC 2072 says that the origin and essence of laughter is nothing but "the affection of truth. . .from which comes gladness of heart and merriment. . . . There is also the affection of good, but this is in the very affection of truth as its soul. The affection of good which is in the rational does not display itself by means of laughter, but by means of a certain joy and consequent pleasurable delight" (*Ibid.*)

What is expressed here is *sheer joy* — joy and happiness that Isaac is born. Sarah had longed for a son, but she was far too old, as was Abraham. How could a child be born to them? But it happened by a Divine miracle. In one sense, nothing could make them happier in their lives upon earth. Their dreams and hopes were fulfilled. Sarah's laughter was not the laughter of contempt. It had within it, symbolically, the joy of the affection of good.

What does the boy Jesus feel when this Divine ability is born to Him? As His love is higher than all other loves, so is His joy at this birth. He sees the rational truths that can save us.

The infant Isaac grew and was weaned, symbolizing the further perfecting and development of the Lord's newborn Divine rationality and also its separation from the merely human reasoning abilities (AC 2645). Abraham and Sarah — the good and truth within the Lord — are married in a new sense with the procreation and birth of Isaac. **The child's weaning called for a great feast, a joyous spiritual feast of celebration.**

At this feast, Ishmael mocked Isaac. Lower reasoning mocks Divine truth; therefore it must be separated. Our lower or natural rational is a blatant doubter. It mocks almost everything worthwhile and substitutes self-appreciation. The Lord sees clearly at this stage that the merely human reasoning in His own maternal heredity has to be banished. This is what Sarah (the Divine Truth) asked. **She asked that Ishmael be banished.**

Abraham loved Ishmael, and he found it very hard at first to banish him and his mother Hagar. Jesus feels "grief from love" (AC 2660) at the thought of banishing the merely human rational. This is not because He loves the false reasoning of this lower rational, but rather because He sees that this kind of reasoning is so much a part of the human race, and has been since the fall of the Most Ancient Church, a people symbolized by Adam and Eve. The people of the Most Ancient Church were led primarily by celestial love and perception. But the Ancient Church, symbolized by those who came after the great flood in Genesis 7, embodied a new kind of people who needed to be led primarily by truth rather than love. The false reasoning of the lower rational, symbolized by Ishmael, is inscribed on every person since the fall of the Most Ancient Church, including each one of us even today. Jesus comes on earth to save this very kind of person (AC 2661). But this kind of person, in order to achieve human warmth and light, must also banish Ishmael-thinking as the primary guide to life. The boy Jesus then goes through a change of state in His thinking about this separation. He sees the inner need for this basic change (AC 2664), and His grief ends.

In the Word or Bible, when one series ends, the same character can take on a new meaning or symbolism. This is so now with Ishmael. Ishmael has so far represented the first or lower reasoning ability, the "wild-ass" reasoning that is to be separated. But once Hagar and Ishmael are separated from the rest of Abraham's family, Ishmael represents the merely spiritual (not celestial) church, or the church that is led by truth as opposed to being led by love (AC 2669).

Jesus sees that the spiritual person, of the spiritual church, needs the support of affirmative human concepts and outer facts. These help him to comprehend doctrine and make it valid in his daily thinking and reflecting. We see much in human literature, in novels like Tolstoy's *War and Peace*, in works of history, and psychological studies like M. Scott Peck's *Further on the Road Less Traveled*, that support and strengthen our faith.

The saving of Ishmael and Hagar from sure death in the wilderness now follows in Genesis 21. God was with Ishmael, and he "became a shooter of the bow" (Gen. 21:2), an archer. The person of the spiritual church defends himself with the arrows of truth. He receives enlightenment from the Lord's Divine Human and this Human saves him (AC 2711). As a boy, Jesus read the story of Hagar and Ishmael and saw these things within it, and it brought Him inner consolation.

Chapter Ten

THE LORD'S MOST GRIEVOUS AND INMOST TEMPTATIONS

THE NEAR SACRIFICE OF ISAAC
GENESIS 22

+ **God tells Abraham to sacrifice Isaac as a burnt offering.**

+ **Abraham nearly sacrifices Isaac, but an angel of Jehovah stops him and a ram is sacrificed instead.**

Isaac was the fulfillment of Jehovah's promise to Abraham. He had been born, circumcised, and in due time weaned from Sarah his mother. Ishmael the mocker has been separated, and the Divine rational is now with Jesus — in its early stages.

The hells are aware of this event, and with their venom they are marshalling to fight against this young rational and, if possible, destroy it (AC 2764, 2819). If they succeed, the Lord's mission on earth will be defeated.

Abraham represents the Divine Love in Jesus in His human essence (AC 2816, 2795). Isaac here is the young Divine rational with limited vision (AC 2795:2). The attack is about to happen. **God called Abraham to take "your son, your only one, whom you love, even Isaac, and get to the land of Moriah, and offer**

**him there for a burnt-offering upon one of the mountains which
I will tell you of" (Gen. 22:2).**

God was calling Abraham to sacrifice his son whom he loved.
There is great significance in the fact that God asks Abraham to
sacrifice "your son, your only one." Isaac pictures Jesus as to the
Divine Human rational level, and He is the "only one in the universe by which He was to save humankind" (AC 2773).

The word "sacrifice" comes from two Latin words, *facere* and
sacra, which combine to mean "to make sacred." Interiorly, this
story reflects a decision in the Lord not to *kill* His new Divine
rational level, but to *sanctify* or *purify* it. This purification would
indeed involve death, but only the death of rational thinking within
Jesus that is limited instead of Infinite.

The historical character named Abraham must have felt despair
at God's command to sacrifice his only son, though it would not
have seemed strange to him. Human sacrifice was prevalent in surrounding cultures at that time.

However, there is no description of despair or any similar emo-
tion on the part of Abraham in Genesis 22. In the literal story,
Abraham hears the word of God and carries it out with no protest.
This is because Abraham represents the internal love of Jesus, and
Jesus saw and recognized that this sanctification <u>must</u> take place in
His new rational level or there would be no hope for humankind.

This sanctification could be accomplished only by means of
severe temptations. Why would these temptations strike the new
Divine Rational with such venom? Why do they come now, while
Jesus is still so young?

When Jesus was born into the world, the "Truth Divine" or
deeper truth within the Word of God was no longer acknowledged
(AC 2813). Instead, religious leaders focused on the literal words
of Scripture, with no interest in deeper Divine meanings. The literal words of Scripture could not remain alive without the presence
of deeper truth, any more than a body can remain alive without the

presence of a soul. Only by bringing Divinity to rational thinking could Jesus establish truly rational thinking into the life of religion. In this way, He makes it possible for us to see and understand deeper truth in the Word of God. In this way, He creates a new link between Himself and human beings, between heaven and earth.

The hells recognize how crucial to the salvation of humankind this new Divine Rational level in young Jesus is, and react accordingly. Jesus must prepare for their severe assaults, and this is described in the arrangements that Abraham makes before his journey to the land of Moriah. Where the story says, **"God did tempt Abraham,"** the celestial or inmost meaning is that young Jesus allows Himself to be tempted. He knows that these most grievous temptations, which have no parallel in the life of any other person that has ever lived, will more closely join His human essence with His Divine Essence. Through them He will come nearer to achieving His goal on earth.

There is an amazing tapestry of interconnection in the stories of the Word and in the internal meaning and its Divine interweaving (AC 2775). The land of Moriah symbolizes a place of temptation. It is one of the mountains on which Jerusalem is built — in fact the eastern height of the city. Isaac is nearly sacrificed on this mountain. Later in history, after King David's sin of numbering the people without Divine command, a plague struck the Israelites, a plague that from Divine intervention stopped at the threshing-floor of Araunah the Jebusite on this same Mount Moriah. Many centuries later, Jesus Himself endured here the extremity of His final temptation. And as late as 1967 another war was fought at this very site. It is, perhaps, appropriate that the "wailing wall" is right here.

So the land of Moriah represents a state of severe trials. Yet within, another state was strongly present. The destination was **"one of the mountains which I will tell you of"** (Gen. 22:2). A mountain signifies Divine Love (AC 2777), and with Jesus, it is His love for our salvation.

This love for others and for their salvation transcends the dread of facing temptations. It is a love that is strongly present throughout this ordeal, although it is not always felt clearly by young Jesus, who is not yet fully Divine.

Abraham prepares for his journey. That he rises early in the morning symbolizes that Jesus prepares for His temptations in a state of peace, knowing that they must happen in order to achieve His goal of salvation. **After three days of preparation and travel, Abraham catches sight of his destination.** "Three" symbolizes completeness. When Jesus' preparation is complete, He enters into the land of "Moriah." The temptation itself is now very near.

Abraham and Isaac went on ahead, without the servants, walking towards the mount. Isaac carried the wood for the offering, and Abraham carried the fire and a knife. The wood is the merit, that is, the recognition by Jesus that He will fight from His own Divine inner power. The fire and knife are the good of love and the truth of faith that He takes with Him into battle (AC 2798). The wood is genuine merit with Isaac, but the fire and knife (the love and the truth) are with Abraham, the Divine Love in the Lord's human essence.

Isaac accompanied his father in innocent trust and love. Before our own temptations, the Lord secretly elevates us into states of warmth and tranquility, even of innocence. This gives us strength to face the trials that follow. This also stands as a challenge to the hells, which, perceiving these states, wish to attack and destroy. So the Lord as a youth, going in spirit to Mount Moriah, is elevated into interior peace and compassion (AC 2786). His young rational is strengthened.

In the story in Genesis, **Isaac did not know that he himself was to be sacrificed: "Behold the fire and the wood; and where is the lamb for a burnt-offering?" (Gen. 22:7)** These words touch our hearts. In the celestial sense, they go even more deeply. The young Divine rational, in a state of limited truth, asks the Divine itself, "Where are those in the human race who are to 'be sancti-fied' or who are to be saved? (see AC 2805). Where are the good people that I may save? I don't see any."

All of the Lord's temptations focused on humankind — here on the youthful Jesus' tender love for us. But His rational mind is still in very limited truth — a state in which things are not clear to Him. In His outward confusion, He cannot see how humankind can be rescued. He despairs.

To Isaac's question Abraham replied: "God will see for Himself the lamb for a burnt-offering." This means that the *Divine Human* which was being developed would provide those who are to be sanctified or saved. This is a Divine answer to young Jesus' prayer. **Together Abraham and Isaac walk on to the mountain,** closer in heart to each other than before (AC 2808).

Within Jesus, the celestial love in His rational that is striving to fulfill His mission now undergoes frightening temptation. This love in His human essence is not yet glorified; it is still finite and bound by appearances (AC 2813). A picture of this is **the boy Isaac, bound upon the altar, with his father raising a knife to kill him.** His rational level is bound (AC 2813, 2814).

Imagine the love and fear in Isaac. He loved his father. Yet his father was about to sacrifice him! The Divine Itself would never, never sacrifice the youthful rational. But the inmost love in this youthful rational, the love of saving humankind, seems about to be destroyed. It seems impossible for the new rational to fulfill its mis-sion. Jesus' love sees from limited truth — truth not genuine enough to see Divine reality (AC 6371, 2813).

Looking from the appearances in this still limited rational (AC 2814), and with the hells viciously attacking, the youthful Jesus feels helpless. He lies upon the wood of the altar, bound and appar-ently about to be destroyed. Jesus' agony at this time is beyond our bearing. The hells are attempting to kill the young rational. It seems to the boy Jesus at the height of this temptation that He will fail.

The hells maliciously attack with their rejection of the deep, inner truth that will save humankind. They inject into Him the message that no one will want to think about deeper truth, no one will want to accept His salvation, that a "lamb" will never be found for a sacrifice, or "sanctifying." As is the love, so is the despair. If our inmost loves are tempted to despair, we are in utter pain. So it is here, with the young Jesus. Something dies in Him then. But what dies is *not* what is Divine (AC 2818)!

Jesus feels terrible despair. But, instead of yielding in this despair, He endures, and a miracle happens. First, "whatever was from the merely human" rational level dies (AC 2818). What despaired in Him dies. In its place is born a higher rational, a Divine rational, that can clearly see the possibility of salvation for all people. This part of Him becomes "the Son of God," the Divine Human.

We bow before this miracle; it is part of the heart of the glorification or the process of Jesus' becoming one with the Divine. Briefly, Jesus finds He <u>cannot</u> from His former limitations save humankind. These limitations involved severe doubts as to whether human beings would ever have interest in the inner truth in the Scriptures, which can lead them directly to God. These doubts He yields up; these die. In resisting and conquering the hells that reject inner truth in the Scriptures, Jesus frees the minds of all people to seek Divine Rational Truth.

What takes the place of former doubts within Jesus, a new level in the Divine Rational glorified, this *can* save us. Out of temptation comes victory. Now from His Divine Human in His glorified rational level, He can *see* the possible reception within humankind and begin to offer salvation. A true rational replaces one that was bound. Isaac is freed from the altar.

For us, true humanity begins in the inmost of our rational. For Jesus the *Divine Human* begins in the inmost of His now glorified Divine Rational. No wonder the hells tried to destroy this great step into Divinity, but they failed.

Out of this temptation — Abraham's nearly sacrificing Isaac — comes something wonderful (AC 2776). Before His birth on earth, the Lord had communication with people here through His highest or celestial kingdom and through an angel spokesman from this heaven. This was sufficient for the earliest or Most Ancient and Ancient Churches and even for the Hebrew and Jewish Churches, although in a less effective way. Finally, all hope of reaching humankind was almost gone. The time had come for the Lord to be born on earth (see TCR 109).

This communication of the Supreme Divine with human beings before His Advent — through the highest angels — is "strictly to be called the *Human Divine*" (AC 2814), (italics added). The term the "Human Divine" involves a limitation in the Lord's power to be with humankind. He Himself was not yet present in His own Divine Human. He needed to work through the angels, and this limited His power to save and redeem (see TCR 109).

There is an ancient prophecy that spoke of this. "The scepter shall not be removed from Judah, nor a lawgiver from between his feet, even until Shiloh comes" (Gen. 49:10), (AC 6371). "Judah" represents the celestial kingdom and the Human Divine.

But this is changed when Shiloh comes. Shiloh is the Lord Incarnate, having been born on earth and then Glorified in His Human, or made one with the Divine. This temptation on Mt. Moriah speaks within of the coming of "Shiloh."

"And the angel of Jehovah called unto him out of heaven, and said, 'Abraham, Abraham,' and he said, 'Here I am' " **(Gen. 22:11).** This calling by the angel, actually by the Divine itself, would have been most gentle and yet a thing of wonder. It stops the temptation from continuing any longer (AC 2822).

"And He said, 'Put not forth your hand upon the boy, and do not do anything unto him; for now I know that you fear God, and you have not withheld your son, your only one, from Me' " **(Gen. 22:12).** This is liberation from the temptation. The tenderest love was under attack at Moriah. This liberation brought greatest joy. The inmost love of the boy Jesus is moved with delight, because those He feared would be lost can now be saved! It would be akin to that incredible feeling of joy when a major war is over and peace finally comes, or to the freedom felt when prisoners of such a war step out of their cells, liberated.

The Lord provided a ram for the sacrifice. The ram represents all those of the spiritual church or genius. To sacrifice the ram here means to sanctify — to save. By the glorification of His Divine rational, the Lord is now able to save all those who are spiritual from the time of this glorification onwards. In addition, this same degree of glorification opens salvation to all the good people in the world who are represented by the families of Nahor in Haran, mentioned at the end of Genesis 22. These are all the good Gentiles on earth.

Jesus liberates the spiritual people and sanctifies them. That is, as the ram was freed from the thicket, so spiritual people are given the means to escape from mental and spiritual entanglement in merely earthly knowledge. The Lord shows them the way to their rebirth, to their reformation and regeneration. This way is first shown in the New Testament, but then is fully unfolded in the Writings of Swedenborg. The "glory in the clouds" is revealed (HH 1), and now the era of true science is gradually dawning. The two foundations of truth (SE 5709), the Word and nature, will meet and support each other.

"A ram behind, caught in a thicket" (Gen. 22:13). It is very easy for us to get caught in the thicket of knowledges. The various disciplines of the sciences and arts can easily *not* liberate but entangle our thinking, in facts or apparent facts and conflicting theories. With many students, the sciences and arts of higher education do not lead to an opening of the mind to the reality of the Lord. Instead they lead to entanglement and often to the negative view that there is no God and that we are animals. The ram is often caught, behind, helpless. The Lord is fully aware of this weakness. In the temptation at Mount Moriah and in the victory, He gives us the means of liberation and true freedom. Jesus has brought Divinity to the rational level of human thinking, making it possible for rationality to be used as a tool in a path to God.

After the temptation and victory at Moriah, the Lord can see that now salvation can come not only to the spiritual, but also to all good people throughout the earth. The vision of the boy Jesus, that so many can be saved, can bring a warmth and breadth to our own concepts of who can be saved. We can see the offering of salvation to the millions of good gentiles throughout the earth.

The account of the near sacrifice of the boy Isaac and his rescue by the angel of Jehovah symbolically marks the end of Jesus' whole childhood. A major step in the glorification is accomplished. The Divine rational is firmly established.

Now the Divine Rational must be enriched, and this is pictured through the death of Sarah in the next chapter. How does a death lead to enrichment? This will be shown through the inner meaning of the next step of the Divine story we are following.

Chapter Eleven

THE ENRICHMENT OF JESUS' RATIONAL

THE DEATH OF SARAH
GENESIS 23

+ **Sarah dies of old age.**
+ **Abraham asks the sons of Heth, in the land of Canaan, for a burial plot and they give him one.**
+ **Sarah is buried.**

As a boy in Egypt, and later in Nazareth, Jesus is taught directly by His Soul, Jehovah. He learns by outer knowledges from the Word but also by streams of inner perceptions from His Soul. The effect on Jesus is expressed in the 119th Psalm, under the Hebrew letter "Mem":

"Oh how I love Your law! It is my meditation all the day. You, through Your commandments, make me wiser than my enemies; for they are ever with me. I have more understanding than my teachers, for Your testimonies are my meditation. I understand more than the ancients, because I have kept Your precepts. I have restrained my feet from every evil way, that I may keep Your word. I have not departed from Your judgments, for You Yourself have taught me. How sweet are Your words to my taste, sweeter than honey to my mouth! Through Your precepts I get understanding; therefore I hate every false way" (Psalm 119: 97-104).

Now in Chapter 23 of the Genesis story comes the death of Sarah, Abraham's beloved wife. To us this suggests feelings of sorrow, but the death of Sarah is not a tragedy in the celestial sense of the story. Death here has a different meaning, as it does for the angels who are eternally and delightfully alive, and do not know what physical death is (AC 2916). In this inner story of Jesus' life Sarah's death represents a further raising and enrichment of the Divine rational (AC 2904). The Divine Truth inflowing into Jesus' Divine rational is newly effective, newly empowered. The Lord, then only a boy in age but a full adult spiritually, does not feel sadness but a resurrection within Himself, a new source of the power to save.

The Divine rational is established, surviving devastating temptations. The Divine Human itself is now living and present in interior thoughts and affections in Jesus. His focus in this state is on the saving of humankind. He inevitably looks to the future, first to the sorrow at negative states that would attack the Christian Church, in which the Trinity would be separated into three gods, and then to the promise and joy of a New Church to be born and established, based on the reception of His Divine Human, in which the Trinity is unified (see TCR 791).

In order that he might bury Sarah's body, Abraham requests a sepulchre from the sons of Heth, in whose land he then dwells. Although in the inner story Sarah's death is not a tragedy, Abraham himself feels great sorrow. **The sons of Heth answer his request with compassion. They wish to help him, to ease his grief. Ephron offers his sepulcher to Abraham.**

There are many levels of meaning to this story. In the internal historical sense Sarah's death may be taken as a prophecy of the end of the first Christian Church, which occurred when all charity and faith had disappeared (AC 2908). Jesus on earth foresees that this will happen, and Abraham's grief over Sarah's death pictures His grief over the death of this Christian Church. Such as is the love, such is the grief. The Lord's love is for the salvation of the human race, and instead of this He foresees a spiritual death. We cannot know grief like this, but its analogy is the earthly death of a conjugial partner. It is devastating.

In this chapter (Genesis 23), the sons of Heth represent "those with whom there was to be a new spiritual church" (AC 2913). These people are open to the Lord and can be regenerated. A "sepulcher" here means not death, but rather rebirth and regeneration (AC 2916). Many in the world are open to regeneration, to rising up out of a spiritually dead state. To the angels, the words **"I will bury my dead"** have nothing to do with physical death. Rather they mean that the <u>Lord</u> "would come forth and rise again from the night in which they were" (AC 2917). "Burying" is to rise again.

Those who will receive the future "New Church" or new understanding about God into their minds will receive the Lord in His Divine Human with kindness and open hearts. Ephron signifies these especially. To Jesus in His early adult age, when the Divine rational has initially been established, His future reception by this New Church moves Him. This is the ultimate hope of His incarnation and glorification: that He will be more and more fully received by a future widespread human understanding and love that will become the crown of all churches.

Regeneration is a process, a step-by-step ascent toward the Lord. The particulars in this story about the sons of Heth show this gradual process of rebirth in the future groups of people who will receive and live the new understanding and love that will be called the New Church. They show how these future people will gradually discover the Lord, and then go through stages of mediate good, including merit, until at last they receive the Lord completely, and from the heart come to ascribe all good and truth to Him. This promise also gives the Lord joy. The cave of Machpelah, where Sarah was buried, may have a sad connotation naturally, but in the internal sense, it speaks of resurrection, of a rediscovery of the Lord upon this earth. It has within it the wonder of the Lord's sepulcher in Jerusalem, from which He rose at Easter fully glorified. It is a resurrection in joy.

INNER UNION OF LOVE AND WISDOM IN THE DIVINE HUMAN
REBEKAH AND ISAAC
GENESIS 24

- ✦ Abraham has his servant travel to Mesopotamia, to the city of Nahor, to find a wife for Isaac among Abraham's family in his homeland.

- ✦ The servant is led by Jehovah to find Rebekah, who is Abraham's niece.

- ✦ Rebekah consents to come back with the servant of Abraham, and Isaac and Rebekah are married.

Genesis next tells of Abraham's wish that his son Isaac find a wife, one that comes from the land of Abraham's origin (Gen. 24). He commissions his trusted servant to travel to the home of his brother Nahor and to find a wife for Isaac there. The servant wonders what he should do if the woman is unwilling to come. Should he take Isaac to her for the marriage?

Abraham replies no, he should not take Isaac there. For the God who had led Abraham to Canaan would "send His angel before you, and you shall take a woman for my son Isaac from there" (Gen. 24:6,7).

The servant is the natural level of Jesus, or His "everyday" mind that takes in outer knowledge (AC 3019). This is subservient to His Divine Love, just as the servant carries out the bidding of his master. Now that the Divine Rational level (Isaac) is fully established, it must join with compatible truth that will come from natural-level knowledge. Jesus wishes to go through the process that we humans go through, that is, to learn knowledge from outside of us, and join it with rational thinking so that it actually becomes truth within us.

From His inner love (Abraham), Jesus sees the need for Divine Truth, a "wife," to come into His rational level, and all truth must start with an *affection* for truth – an interest that will lead to truth. This affection is what Jesus must now search for.

But Jesus knows that He must not choose just any affection to bring truth to His Divine Rational level. **Abraham tells the servant not to choose from any of the surrounding Canaanite women.** This symbolizes the Lord's inner awareness that He is still surrounded by impure affections in His finite maternal heredity. He knows that He must travel elsewhere with His search (AC 3024).

The "angel" that would go before the servant signifies "the Divine Providence" (AC 3039). "Conjugial love" or true and spiritual marriage love is "above every love" (CL 64) with the angels of heaven and the people of the church. It is a gift that is the highest reception of the Lord in two hearts, the husband's and the wife's. The Divine Providence works, above all else, for the protection and establishment of the conjugial in each person. The Lord sends His angel to lead to this inmost love, and to establish it forever.

Conjugial love has its origin in the union of truth and love in each person. When truth and love are lived by both, a man and woman may be led to the initial discovery of each other as potential eternal partners. With Jesus Himself, there is to be a conjunction of truth with good on His rational plane, where His Divine Human begins. This is the potent origin of our own conjugial hopes — our hopes for an eternally happy marriage. Unless this conjunction between the Rebekah and Isaac of His mind takes place within Jesus, there will be no hope of conjugial love for the people on earth.

Abraham's servant is led to the city of Nahor and comes to a well there. This pictures how Jesus travels into the knowledges related to doctrine or religious principles that He has acquired for Himself. These kinds of knowledges are symbolized by the city of Nahor (AC 3052). Jesus stands ready now to learn from doctrinal principles about real truth that He can make His own on a rational level (AC 3013). He waits for an appropriate affection, a "woman," to show itself, and lead Him into deeper learning. This affection for truth that Jesus looks for must be "a virgin," innocent and pure from falsity.

In the literal story, the servant prays that Jehovah will lead Isaac's future wife to the well and that he, the servant, will know her by her offering him water and then offering his camels water also. Almost incredibly, this takes place. Rebekah, a beautiful virgin, comes out to get water, and when the servant asks her for a drink, she gives him water, and then also waters his camels. He asks her who she is, and she replies; " 'I am the daughter of Bethuel the son of Milcah, whom she bare unto Nahor'. . . . And the man [the servant] bent himself, and bowed himself to Jehovah. And he said, 'Blessed be Jehovah the God of my lord Abraham . . . . Jehovah has led me to the house of my lord's brothers' " (Gen. 24:24-27, selections).

"Rebekah," beautiful and pure, is the innocent affection for or interest in doctrinal knowledge that Jesus has been searching for (AC 3080). He allows this affection to instruct Him, and it enlightens Him, as Rebekah quenches the thirst of the servant and his camels.

When we are young, we are taught doctrinal concepts, such as "God takes care of us, all the time." To our childhood minds this is a wonderful thought, and it fills us with affection. Later, when we develop rational thinking, we can go back to these innocent, beautiful affections for doctrinal concepts. If we can then take them in and "marry" them to spiritual rational thinking, they will become real truth for us. "God takes care of us" will no longer be just a nice thing someone told us. It makes <u>sense</u> to us. We see it in life and believe it for ourselves. It becomes our own and is transformed, as the water was changed to wine at the marriage in Cana (Luke 2:9).

And so it is for Jesus. He finds within His natural mind a pure and innocent love for doctrinal concepts. He will take this and marry it to His rational level. There it will no longer be just an affection. It will become Divine Truth in His Divine Rational level. Rebekah will no longer be a beautiful virgin; she will be a beautiful wife.

In the literal story, when the servant arrives at the house of Laban and Bethuel, he is offered food and hospitality, but he does not eat until he has told his full story to these two. When he finishes his recounting, he asks them their response to the idea of Rebekah becoming Isaac's wife. They reply: "The word has gone forth from Jehovah; we cannot speak unto you evil or good. Behold, Rebekah is before you; take her, and go, and let her be the woman of your lord's son, as Jehovah has spoken" (Gen. 24:50,51).

When asked if she will accompany the servant back to the land of Canaan to marry Isaac, Rebekah answers: "I will go" (Gen. 24:58). When they arrive at Abraham's home, the servant tells Rebekah that it is Isaac who is coming to meet them. She willingly comes into Sarah's tent, and "Isaac loved her, and he was comforted after his mother" (Gen. 24:67).

This is the fulfillment of the story about the angel's leading Rebekah and Isaac to each other. Consent is given, and love comes from the Lord. Today there is so much cynicism about marriage and much doubt about the possibility that marriages can last. Here, very simply, the Lord says, "Yes, conjugial love is possible, and this is the story of how it starts. The Lord sends His angel."

This gift is not possible unless in the supreme sense Rebekah is found and led to Isaac. This Divine union is essential to the birth of conjugial love with every human being. Isaac is the Divine good in the Lord's newly established Divine rational (AC 3210). This good with Him is key: from good or love comes all else that is truly alive, filled with buoyancy and potential joy. But good cannot be effective alone. To be complete it needs union with truth. In the inner story we have the betrothal of Divine truth with Divine Good and then the marriage of these two (AC 3210, 3211, and 3212).

Of this Divine conjunction we read: **"And Isaac was comforted after his mother"** (Gen. 24:67), **that is, after the death of Sarah**. He loved Rebekah, and with her found inner fulfillment and happiness. These words about Isaac's being comforted signify "a new state" (AC 3212). In the Lord there is a conjunction within that changes His life on earth, and that brings the Divine Human fully into being.

This marriage of Isaac and Rebekah represents a whole new state in Jesus Christ on earth. Earlier His rational was glorified as to good, but now with the union with Rebekah, He is glorified also as to truth (AC 3212). This process of glorification can be understood better if we realize that our own regeneration is somewhat like it, but on a lower, limited level. As we struggle through temptations, the Lord will gradually change our inner selfish and domineering nature. He enables us to become more loving, thoughtful, and compassionate towards others. Our faces and bodies don't change; our inner natures do. We become new persons in our reactions to people and life situations.

The disciples Peter, James, and John see a deep inner change with the Lord when, after putting off His finite maternal heredity, Jesus is "transfigured" before them on the mountain, and His face shines as the sun. So we too may be reborn, touched by His love.

The *full* glorification within Jesus Christ is yet to come. But this union of truth and good within His rational mind is a significant step towards that full transformation. It foreshadows the complete marriage of the Divine and Human within the Lord.

BIRTH OF THE DIVINE NATURAL

ESAU AND JACOB
GENESIS 25

+ **Abraham dies of old age.**

+ **Isaac and Rebekah have twins, Jacob and Esau.**

+ **Esau was the firstborn, but Jacob takes the birthright from Esau by withholding food from his starving older brother until he swears to sell his birthright to him.**

There is an innocent side to each of us, instilled in our infancy and childhood. To this side of our nature the Divine Natural is our Savior. The "Divine Natural" is the Lord present with us on the level in which we live day by day. In Genesis 25 we see the birth of this Divine Natural in the birth of Jacob and Esau.

Isaac, the Divine rational, is the Lord coming to our higher rational, our spiritual thinking. Early in adulthood we have an idealistic passion for spiritual rational thinking, and this is where we especially need the Lord. When we find our faith, when our rational is open to the wonders of the teachings in the Word of God, our lives are changed. Through this growing intellectual faith we develop an inner orientation that looks to heaven and to the Lord. Our purposes in life are established in response to Him.

As we grow older and perhaps are married and have children, our perspectives change. We often focus more on life's challenges and problems and less on spiritual thinking. Our selfishness begins to intrude in our marriages or our hopes for marriage. We can become colder and less responsive. We strive to succeed in our work, to find self-fulfillment in our homes, and to acquire money and status. Good vacations might mean more to us than our regeneration. We may not have true concern for others, and our idealism is left behind. We are not alive to the Lord. The focus has shifted from rational idealism to the natural plane of life.

We may slowly begin to wonder, "Where is the Lord of our early adult life?" As time passes and we begin to achieve some of our goals (or fail to achieve them) we become quietly aware that something is wrong. We are not deeply happy. We aren't finding the happiness in life that we anticipated. This loss of meaning in life may last for some time, until we finally experience an awakening, a genuine desire to find the Lord again. Now we would like to find Him where we live, on the daily plane of life.

The Lord came on earth and glorified His natural so that He could reach us and help us change our hearts in our day-to-day lives. On His own level, after the establishment of the Divine rational, He turns to a new focus. He begins to focus on His natural level. In His heredity through Mary He finds the very problems of which we speak. The Divine is not yet present there, not strongly operative in this heredity. He finds coldness, a rejection of inflowing Divine life. How He handles this strong challenge, aggravated by the venom and malice of the hells, is the key to finding the Lord in *our* daily lives. The Divine Natural is our Rescuer, Who can change what is dead or humdrum into moments that have eternal meaning.

Swedenborg's Writings reveal that the natural level "receives truths much later, and with greater difficulty, than the rational" (AC 3321:3). In our natural minds is a quality that opposes the

Lord, which fights against Him. It leads us into a darkness of mind (AC 3322:1,2).

As we mature beyond early adult age, we find in ourselves barriers to heavenly life. What we don't want to admit is that we have goals that are not heavenly. They are in our daily lives, and they are awfully potent. These goals have in them contempt for the Divine. However, on the higher plane of our hearts and minds, the rational plane, we still do believe in the Lord and love Him. A war is going to take place then, right in our hearts. Esau and Jacob, the twin sons of Isaac and Rebekah, speak spiritually to this quandary, and the celestial meaning of their story will show us the path.

Isaac was forty years old when he married Rebekah. At first she was barren, but Isaac prayed to the Lord for mercy, and in time Rebekah conceived. Two sons struggled within her womb, and she enquired of Jehovah: " 'Why am I thus?'

"And Jehovah said unto her, 'Two nations are in your womb, and two peoples shall be separated from your body, and the one people shall prevail over the other people, and the elder shall serve the younger.' And her days were fulfilled to bring forth, and behold twins were in her womb. And the first came forth red all over like a hairy garment, and they called his name Esau. And after that came forth his brother, and his hand laid hold on Esau's heel, and he called his name Jacob; and Isaac was a son of sixty years when she bare them" (Gen. 25:20-26, selections).

In the inner story, the conception and birth of Jacob and Esau are the conception and birth of the Divine natural. The good-oriented side of the Divine natural is Esau. The truth-oriented side is Jacob (AC 3232). These births with Jesus are to change not only Him but us too – not our rational visions and ideals, but how heaven can actually come to us here in our homes and our work and our recreation. Without these births we would be like animals in our lower minds. Now, from the Lord, we can become human.

Right at the birth we glimpse how this change happens. **"The elder shall serve the younger" (Gen. 25:23).** After our rational faith is established and our focus has shifted to living in this natural world, we start to desire spontaneity. We look for goodness to come to us openly, effortlessly, with a natural ease. At first it seems to. But then we find what the Lord found before us: that the Esau quality, good in the natural, is at first plagued by hereditary tendencies to evil. The Lord found good in the natural "so far as it was from [His] mother was imbued with hereditary evil" (AC 3599).

Esau represents the Divine natural as to good, and Jacob the Divine natural as to truth. Within us, Esau is "good" that is unrefined in our natural or daily lives and that actually has much selfishness within it. Jacob on the other hand is truth in the natural. This consists mainly of knowledges from the Word that we believe are true. But we see these knowledges and truths only in a limited way. So initially both Esau and Jacob have strong limitations. This is what the Lord finds too, in His heredity through Mary (AC 3599:2).

Jesus knows that the way in which He will handle these two forces in His natural level is a key to the future salvation of humankind. Regeneration, truly becoming an angel, is a process that must happen on the natural level with us. Here we need the Lord, and we need Him desperately.

Through many states we try to put Esau first, because this seems so right; it seems like the true order of creation, to go with your instincts of what feels good and right. It would be, too, if there were no hereditary evil. But since, before we are spiritually reborn, our instincts are tainted with selfishness, we cannot trust them to lead. Jacob (truth) must come first for now, because true ideas must instruct our developing will. This is not the ideal order. This is clear even in the story, where **Jacob *steals* both Esau's birthright and his blessing.** Jacob represents knowledge of truth from the Word that we compel ourselves to put into our lives. The

Esau in us caves in to evil, but applied truth brings order and puts us on the path to the Lord.

In order to regenerate we need to compel ourselves by free choice to obey truth for a long time. This is what reforms the natural level. We change and progress through self-discipline, with the Lord's help. We may try to deny this, but we will find that it is true. We may still try to put Esau first, and then find it doesn't work. We have within us too much hereditary inclination to contempt, to a sense of superiority, even to adultery. We need the help of Divine truth, and we need it badly.

Genesis speaks of Esau's coming in from the field, "and he was weary" (Gen. 25:29). That he was weary "signifies a state of combat" (AC 3318). Temptations are the key means of change and rebirth (*Ibid.*). Our hereditary loves of self and the world distort and harden the very vessels in the mind that would otherwise receive heavenly influx. Temptations order and soften us, turning us toward the Lord and away from stubborn self-love. Much in our natural level of emotions and thoughts is spiritually hard, hard with conceit and arrogance. In order to be reborn, we need softening (see AC 3318). This change brings another, gentler nature to our being, one that includes simplicity and a touch of humility. We then feel love and compassion for others as never before in our adult life.

So with the Lord, who established the path for us, "Jacob" for a time has apparent priority over "Esau." The Lord's process, or "the glorification," needed to proceed through Divine truth to Divine good even in His Natural. In the story of Jacob's life and his final return to the land of Canaan and to Esau, the pathway through truth to good is revealed, and so also for the Lord, our leader, from Divine truth to Divine good.

Think of Jesus as a youth in Nazareth. He has had the most delightful learning experiences as well as severe temptations in childhood. His mind is filled with perceptions and love for Jehovah. He knows His future mission and is preparing for it.

Outwardly, he is an apprentice carpenter with his earthly stepfather. He must have been seen as an extra-ordinary child and youth, loving but not deeply understood.

Yet He is in no way alone. Jehovah and the angels are with Him, and so are Mary and probably still Joseph. But He is finding now the unregenerate natural level He has inherited through Mary. He perceives in this heredity not spontaneous good, but the same need to compel His natural level to order, and then to glorify this level. He must take every feeling and impulse in His natural level and compare it with the truth He has learned from His Divine Soul, Jehovah. If the two are not in agreement, He must subdue this feeling to the higher Truth. Jesus is right with us on this path.

By this means the Lord "altogether changed His human state" (AC 3296:2). He changes it from being human to being Divinely Human (*Ibid.*). By the same process the Lord can change us, in our case from being "dead" to becoming alive, leaving what is old, and coming into what is young and "new" (*Ibid.*).

"And Abraham gave all that he had unto Isaac. . . .And Abraham expired in a good old age, an old man and sated, and was gathered to his peoples" (Gen. 25:5,8). Because Abraham represents the Lord's Divine infancy and then the Divine itself, we feel a sense of sorrow in his passing. But within, in the Divine government and mercy, Abraham's death indicates a major step of progress. The focus in the glorification now shifts to Isaac and then before long to Jacob. Each change represents a further stage in the glorification, the process by which Jesus would become fully Divine, and an extending of the power of the Divine Human to save humankind.

In the broadest sense, we see an aspect of childhood with us until we are thirty. Even contemporary psychology recognizes this. Although adult age is said to start at twenty (AC 10225), a part of us is still in childhood states for another decade or so (see AC 5353). It is in harmony with this that Abraham stayed alive throughout much of Isaac's life. Only a short time after Abraham died, when his representation of the Lord ceased, Jacob and Esau were born. States overlap, and one state becomes rich and full of remains before yielding to the next. **"And Abraham gave all that he had unto Isaac" (Gen. 25:5).**

The Jacob-Laban-Esau stories reveal how the Lord makes self-discipline as easy as possible. It reveals how delights can be maintained despite the need for self-compulsion in regeneration. The truth is that the Lord walks with us every step of the way, even though this is not always evident.

Chapter Thirteen

THE DIVINE RATIONAL IS FULLY BLESSED

JEHOVAH BLESSES ISAAC
GENESIS 26

- ✦ Jehovah appears to Isaac and promises descendants "as the stars of heaven" and that they would be blessed.

- ✦ Isaac tells the men of Gerar that Rebekah is his sister, for the same reason Abraham did earlier.

- ✦ Abimelech, the king of the Philistines in Gerar, discovers Isaac's deception and warns the men of Gerar not to touch Rebekah.

- ✦ Isaac begins to prosper in the land of the Philistines, and the Philistines quarrel with Isaac's herdsmen over access to the well water in the land.

- ✦ Isaac moves to Beersheba, makes peace with Abimelech and is prosperous.

In Genesis 26 Jehovah blesses Isaac. More deeply, the story tells how the Isaac rational with the Lord is enriched, and how the Lord rediscovers truths long since lost on this earth. If He is to order and glorify His natural, the rational within Him also needs further glorification. It must be blessed. The blessing of His Divine rational comes from an even higher level within Himself, from His Soul.

In glorifying His Human, Jesus achieves the power to work through the Word on its every level, to touch and move human hearts and thoughts. It is said that **"Isaac returned, and digged again the wells of water which they had digged in the days of Abraham his father" (Gen. 26:18).** This represents "that the Lord opened those truths which were with the ancients" (AC 3419)! Perhaps the Ancient Word itself comes into His possession from Egypt, and has its deepest celestial meaning opened to Him by His Soul.

In this chapter, once again a patriarch calls his wife his "sister." **"And Isaac said [to the men of Gerar], Rebekah is my sister" (Gen. 26:7).** This symbolizes that Divine truths, represented by Rebekah, are presented through appearances (the "sister" here). The Lord, when He was in the human part of Himself that wasn't yet Divine, was also in the "appearance" of truth (AC 3405). This means that Divine Truth was adapted to the level at which He was able to grasp it at that time. Divine truth itself, in its essence, is above the receiving ability of finite humans, whether living on earth or as angels in heaven, and it was above the receiving ability of the not-yet-glorified Jesus.

But later, Isaac was led to admit that Rebekah was his wife. This has two immediate meanings: first, that Divine truth, which is accommodated to us by the Lord Himself, *is Divine* by virtue of its origin, and thus is a wife, not a sister; and secondly, that the highest or celestial level of the mind can perceive rational revelation to be Divine and of Divine authority. It sees Rebekah as Isaac's wife, whereas the next level down, or the spiritual level of the mind, cannot easily conceive of a rational revelation as being Divine (AC 3394:2,3), but rather thinks of it as merely human, and thus here as a sister.

Jesus Himself was attacked by the illusion that "Rebekah," or the truth He had gained from the Word of God, was only as a sister to Him. His finite maternal heredity instilled the false concept that rational truths inflowing from His Soul are only finite and not Divine. But He sees the horror of this suggestion that comes from His finite heredity, and rejects it. Rebekah as a wife is Divine truth married to Divine good in His rational mind (Isaac). To call such Divine truth a sister is to remove it from the Divine marriage.

In its celestial sense, this chapter reveals that the Isaac rational, the Divine rational with the Lord, is now fully blessed. **Isaac discovers "a well of living waters" (Gen. 26:19).** This is true for Jesus as a youth in Nazareth. The Lord would have it be true for us. Our knowledge of the Word of God, our love for living truths, can broaden and deepen. This prepares the way for a wonderful gift: the rebirth of the natural level within ourselves. If this is reborn, we become "heaven-made."

Chapter Fourteen

THE NATURAL LEVEL OF JESUS TO BE GLORIFIED

THE BLESSING OF JACOB AND ESAU
GENESIS 27

+ Isaac has become very old and blind. He asks Esau to bring him a meal before he dies so that he can bless Esau.

+ Rebekah overhears Isaac's request and has Jacob, disguised as Esau, bring Isaac a meal to deceive him into blessing Jacob.

+ Isaac blesses Jacob. Esau returns, finds out that Jacob has stolen his blessing and begs Isaac for some type of blessing, which he receives.

+ After hearing Esau threaten Jacob's life, Rebekah urges Jacob to flee to Laban, Rebekah's brother, in Haran.

Chapter 27 of Genesis returns to the story of Jacob and Esau and the blessing of each by Isaac their father. Isaac was now "old, and his eyes were dim that he could not see" (Gen. 27:1). Growing "old" in the Word does not mean physical aging; angels do not know what old age is because they are perpetually young. Instead, "old" means "the presence of a new state," (AC

3492) and this chapter deals with a new state in the Lord's natural level.

Jacob stole the blessing that was intended for Esau, and Rebekah helped him to do this. This seems completely wrong. Yet it reflects a truth that we are not born good. We are born with hereditary evil tendencies to overcome. We need to be reborn. Rebirth is necessary if we are to find true happiness in our natural, day-to-day plane of life.

The Lord changed on this plane of life, and so showed the path for how *we can change*. The final goal that Jesus Christ seeks with us is to lead us to become wise infants (wise, but with the trust of an infant), living in the present in our daily natural life and looking to the Lord as our deeply loved Father (AC 3494:2).

In His glorification process, the Lord does not put Esau first. The Esau with Him, the good or love in His natural, is impure from the heredity He took on through Mary. On His path, truth is first in time (AC 3599). He endures the difficulty of self-compulsion by obeying Divine truth. But He sees the end, the goal, and in this is His joy. As a result, He can now establish this same path in the heart of each one of us, and lead us along it if we wish to follow.

We would love to have the good or love in our natural level be spontaneously pure — a wonderful and free guide to our lives. But we discover that this good has hereditary evil tendencies within it. Esau within us must wait to rule until after it has been purified. Jacob must take the lead. Yet Jacob, our concept of truth in the natural, is also limited. It needs education, and purification.

The following song expresses the conundrum about our hearts and our thinking, about wishing for spontaneous good to rule within us, yet finding that it cannot. Truth must lead instead.

> My mind knows You are here
> But my heart,
> Oh my heart is left behind.

I am leaving the door open for You.
Please come through.

My life is an open book
Let the end be written by You.

My hands are in Your hands;
Let them do as You want to.

My spirit longs for You to
Come and share bread and wine.

Come and quench the thirst
That earthly water cannot touch.

Only a cup of Your water of life
Can make me whole.
Heather Childs

Swedenborg's Writings speak about the same subject that this song does: "The natural does not become new, or receive life corresponding to the rational, that is, is not regenerated, except by means of doctrinal things, or the knowledges of good and truth" (AC 3502:2). "Only a cup of Your water of life can make me whole."

Before the door can be opened for the Lord to come through, the heart must be purified. The mind must become new through drinking the water of life. We drink by learning the Lord's truth and living it. Then the heart becomes new, and the Lord can come in to us (AC 3504).

Jacob steals the blessing because the initial blessing in the rebirth of the natural level is by means of truth, represented by

Jacob. That this is <u>not</u> the way the Lord originally created the process of spiritual human development is evident from the fact that Jacob *stole the honor.* Yet Rebekah led the way in this. She represents Divine truth in the rational: a higher truth.

This higher truth knows that the natural can be reborn only through our compelling ourselves to obey the revealed truth (AC 1937). Since this is the reality of our rebirth, the Lord with all His love and tender Providence makes this path as easy and joyful as possible, just as Jacob's father gave him a wonderful blessing.

Inmostly, good is always first. Without the goodness of remains — innocent loves from childhood — in our hearts, we would never be able to compel ourselves to obey the truth. Later, good breaks the yoke of self-compulsion to obey truth. From love we then <u>want</u> to live a good life, and do so freely. Good openly rules, and self-compulsion no longer dominates our lives. **So Isaac was able to tell Esau, after giving Jacob a full and rich blessing: "Upon your sword you shall live, and shall serve your brother [Jacob]; and it shall come to pass, when you shall have the dominion, that you shall break his yoke from upon your neck" (Gen. 27:40).**

The Lord goes through the Jacob/Esau states (AC 3508) while He is in Nazareth. Somehow it is instinctive to think of Jesus Christ as being without any tendencies to evil. Perhaps because we think of Him glorified, we tend to forget that He came on earth to assume a heredity through Mary in order to face and subdue the hells and glorify His Human. And yet, there in Nazareth, Jesus was facing all of the negative thoughts and feelings that we ourselves face. He was working constantly to reject all thoughts and feelings that were not in accord with Divine Love, and thus glorify His human heart into a Divinely Human heart.

In establishing this path, the Lord's purpose was to set our hearts free, so that we will want to do only what is good.

"Bless the Lord, O my soul. And forget not all His benefits:

Who forgives all your iniquities, Who heals all your diseases, Who redeems your life from destruction, Who crowns you with loving-kindness and tender mercies, Who satisfies your mouth with good things, so that your youth is renewed like the eagle's" (Psalm 103: 2-5; see also AC 3610:2).

Chapter Fifteen

THE MEANS TO GLORIFY THE NATURAL

JACOB'S LADDER
GENESIS 28

> ✦ Jacob leaves his father and mother to find a wife from Laban's daughters.
>
> ✦ Esau leaves also, to find a wife from Ishmael's daughters.
>
> ✦ On his journey Jacob has a dream about angels descending and ascending on a ladder to God.

Isaac called Jacob, blessed him, and asked him to travel to Paddan-aram to find a wife from the daughters of Laban. Isaac and Rebekah didn't want Jacob to marry a Canaanite woman. In their hearts they wished he would marry a woman from among their relatives back in the homeland of Haran. Isaac promised that God Shaddai would protect Jacob and that Shaddai would give him the blessing of Abraham.

It is now time for the natural level of Jesus, His "everyday" mind represented by Jacob, to join with outer knowledge that will lead this level to Divinity. Outer knowledge involves simple truths found in the literal stories of the Word, as well as knowledge of how things function in nature, and the outer, everyday dealings among human beings.

But Jesus must not join with outer knowledge that denies the existence of spiritual and celestial truth, symbolized by the Canaanite women (AC 3665:2). He must search for outer knowledge that *admits* the existence of such higher truth, symbolized by the daughters of Laban, because only in this way can He join the natural, everyday mind with the pure and heavenly mind. If He does this, He makes it possible for us to do so as well. Thus, Jacob's travels to find an appropriate wife picture Jesus' journey in the realm of outer knowledge that can lead His natural mind to Divinity.

In the literal story, Jacob prepared for his long journey and left Beersheba. On the first night he camped near Luz, by the border near the Jordan. The sun set, and he took one of the nearby stones and used it for his pillow.

"And he dreamed a dream, and behold a ladder set on the earth, and its head reaching to heaven; and behold the angels of God ascending and descending on it. And behold Jehovah standing upon it; and He said, 'I am Jehovah the God of Abraham your father, and the God of Isaac; the land whereon you lie, to you will I give it, and to your seed. . . .And behold, I am with you, and will keep you wherever you go, and will bring you back to this ground' " (Gen. 28:12-15, selections).

The fact that night was falling represents that now Jesus, conscious in His natural mind, is in an "obscure" state. In our everyday, natural-level consciousness there are countless spiritual issues of which we are only dimly aware. Here in this natural level, Jesus does not have the ability to discern among all the deeper issues that are so clear to His higher levels of consciousness.

Jacob's dream symbolizes something that is revealed to Jesus by His Divine Soul. Jesus is shown that there will indeed be a full and active connection between the outer knowledge in His natural mind and the Divine level of celestial truth and goodness. There will be "infinite and eternal" communication and conjunction between the lowest truths of nature and the Word, and the highest truths of the Divine (AC 3701, 3699). The outer, everyday thoughts, decisions, and actions of Jesus will ascend to seek Divine enlightenment, and Divine enlightenment will flow down into them, shaping and affecting them. This is represented by the angels ascending and descending on the dream ladder that connects heaven and earth.

When Jacob woke up he said, "Surely Jehovah is in this place, and I knew it not." And he was afraid, and said, "How awesome is this place! This is none other than the house of God, and this is the gate of heaven" (Gen. 28:12-17).

Jacob got up, took the stone that he had used for a pillow, and raised it as a pillar. He poured oil on it, marking it as a holy altar, and named the place Bethel, which means "the house of God."

This prophecy that the Divine Soul reveals fills Jesus with awe and enlightenment. Even here, in the obscurity and confusion of natural-level issues, the Divine is present. **"Surely the Lord is in this place, and I knew it not."** Jacob's fear and awe symbolize Jesus' startling realization that the Divine is indeed present in outer, everyday knowledge and life. This realization alters Jesus' natural-level outlook in a sacred way (AC 3718). He sees the presence of Divinity in the natural-level order of life: **"This is none other than the house of God"** (AC 3720). He sees that even the laws of nature can provide a gateway to knowledge of God, only because God is the life force that flows into nature: **"This is the gate of heaven"** (AC 3721).

In this part of Genesis our own natural level is being reborn (representatively) as to its thinking (truth) and as to its love (good). This is done step by step, symbolized by ascending a ladder of life.

104

But first consider the setting that leads up to the dream and its symbolism. Jacob is now the central focus of the story. He represents a natural-level way of thinking (AC 3559:2). Jacob's being sent to Aram or Syria by Isaac is prophetic, for Syria represents the "knowledges of truth" (AC 3664). The ladder's beginning, set on the earth, is the "ultimates of order" (AC 3657). The ultimates of order are plain truths from the Old and New Testaments, such as the Ten Commandments, the stories of creation, of the patriarchs, of the founding of the Israelite nation, of Elijah and Elisha, of the prophets and psalms, of the coming of Jesus Christ and the gospels of the New Testament, and finally the tapestry and beauty of the book of Revelation. Such "ultimates" also include the plain, general truths of the Writings. From these the Lord disposes the intermediates, which are the steps of the ladder ascending upward to him. The intermediates are the levels of emotions, thoughts, and affections in our minds that ascend, as in steps, up to the Lord.

When we ascend a number of steps up the ladder of truth, it enables us to come nearer to the Lord, and enables Him to elevate our daily lives. At first our motives are mixed, having both what is selfish and what is unselfish within. We want to serve and love the Lord, but much of our orientation from heredity looks to self and self-glory (AC 3701:4; AC 3993:9-11). But in time, we perceive a higher rung of truth. We look within and see formerly hidden conceit or pride. This we may shun from our love and obedience to the Lord. The next rung reveals a higher concept of truth, and exposes other lower, selfish motives formerly not perceived as such. Thus we gradually may ascend toward the Lord, who stands at the height or top of this ladder of life. Gradually our natural level changes, and we are *actually* reborn.

All this is made possible because the Lord on earth followed this order. He establishes this ladder of life for us and makes it possible for us to ascend. Doing this brings Him into severe struggles. **Isaac said to Jacob his son, "God Shaddai will bless you" (Gen.**

28:3). God Shaddai represents God's presence during temptations (AC 3667). It is through temptations that Jesus, our Savior, makes His natural level Divine (Lord 33, 34).

How does Jesus Christ begin this process? He turns to the Word, to the Old Testament and perhaps also to the Ancient Word. As a boy He studied this Word in depth (represented by Abram's time in Egypt and also by Jesus' time in Egypt as an infant). Streams of perceptions about the inner meaning of the Word flow into Him from His Soul.

Much later in His life on earth, when it comes time for His natural level to be reborn, He turns again to this outer truth. He reads the Word, understanding celestial levels within it that we scarcely dream of. He applies these transforming truths to His natural. He applies them to His finite maternal heredity to bring about radical changes. He imposes Divine order upon this human in order to transform His life.

Gradually His finite human heredity is put aside as the Word becomes more and more His Being (see TCR 85:2). It seems from the evidence that this is quite a while before His public ministry, long before He is thirty years of age. Who beholds these inner changes? The angels are aware to some extent and are deeply moved. Even Mary — and Joseph too — would be aware of a different sphere about Jesus, a growing gentleness and amazing compassion.

Jacob said of his future: "I [will] return in peace to my father's house" (Gen. 28:21). The Divine natural would become One with His Soul. He would come home and invite us to our own spiritual home.

"Come unto Me, all you that labor and are heavy laden, and I will revive you. Take My yoke upon you, and learn of Me, that I am meek and humble in heart: and you shall find rest for your souls, for My yoke is easy, and My burden light" (Matt. 11:28-30).

Chapter Sixteen

INITIAL STAGES OF GLORIFICATION OF THE NATURAL

JACOB IN HARAN: THE EARLY YEARS
GENESIS 29

+ Jacob journeys to Paddan-aram and meets Laban's daughter Rachel at a well.

+ Jacob loves Rachel and asks Laban for permission to marry her.

+ Laban tricks Jacob into marrying his older daughter, Leah.

+ Laban says Jacob can also marry Rachel if he works for seven more years, which Jacob does.

+ Rachel is unable to have children, but Leah has four: Reuben, Simeon, Levi, and Judah.

Here at a well Jacob met Rachel, who was coming to water her father's sheep. When Jacob found out who she was, he watered her sheep, and then "Jacob kissed Rachel, and lifted up his voice and wept" (Gen. 29:11). Providence had led him to his kindred. Soon Laban, Rachel's father, came to meet

Jacob and took him into his home.

After a month there, Laban asked Jacob how he could reward him for his services on Laban's farm: "And Jacob loved Rachel, and he said, I will serve you seven years for Rachel, your younger daughter" (Gen. 29:18). He faithfully did this, but on the wedding night Laban substituted Leah, the older daughter, as Jacob's bride. When Jacob protested strongly the next morning, Laban said that the custom in this place was that the older daughter must marry first. Jacob agreed to serve for seven more years for Rachel, for his love for her was deep: the first seven years he served for her "were in his eyes as a few days, for the love he had for her" (Gen. 29:20).

Then Rachel became Jacob's wife. "And Jehovah saw that Leah was hated, and He opened her womb, and Rachel was barren" (Gen. 29:31). Leah then had four sons: Reuben, Simeon, Levi and Judah.

In the supreme inner sense of this story this chapter unfolds the beginning of the glorification of the Lord's natural level. Jacob symbolizes the truth applied in the Lord's natural mind and His willingness to *obey* this truth. Finite human qualities within His natural level are seen and cast out in a series of Divinely ordained steps. The preparation for and unfolding of this is in the hands of Jehovah, the Divine and loving Father. **Jacob was led to Haran in Syria.** Syria represents the knowledge needed to lead His natural to become one with the Father.

In Providence Jacob met Rachel, who was "beautiful in form and appearance" (Gen. 29:17). He fell in love, strongly, tenderly. Rachel represents a love of Divine truth that will lead the Lord to glorification. But first came Jacob's marriage to Leah, who represents a love for lower and more external truths. Living by these lower truths prepares for the deeper marriage with Rachel (AC 3758,9).

Laban is the father of both Leah and Rachel. He symbolizes a good that begets loves of truth, loves of the Word. This good is called "corporeal good" (AC 3778:3). Within us, "corporeal good" is the earliest remains or affections of love: celestial qualities of innocence and trust instilled in our infancy. Around this infantile good would be many mistaken childish notions and fallacies (*Ibid.*). But still, the good and innocence are within. These remains are the basis, the foundation, for the desire to be reborn. From these remains come the hope and strong desire to have our natural mind change from being dead to becoming alive and filled with perception and genuine love.

Jesus, in the glorification of His natural, has a similar basis within Himself. We know that the youthful Jesus has remains, for this is taught in the *Arcana Coelestia* (see 4176, 1906). The remains with Jesus, however, are Divine and enable Him to be not merely regenerated but glorified, or fully united with His Divine Soul. These remains are a motivating force in His natural, and bring about an utter transformation there. These are the Lord's Laban qualities, which are allied to His Soul and His spiritual-celestial nature. It takes powerful Divine forces such as these to bring about a change in His hereditary natural, to bring the transformation that will change our world. His strong love of truth in His natural was born of the Laban within Him, His Divine "remains" (AC 1906:4).

The Lord's glorification of His natural was accomplished by means of the Word. **Jacob met Rachel by a well of water.** This is the water of life: the Word itself. **When he met Rachel, he "lifted up his voice and wept" (Gen. 29:11).** These were tears of happiness. This represents the Lord's perception that it truly is the Word, the water of life, that can bring changes to His natural and glorify it.

Jacob loved Rachel, but he was given Leah instead, Leah whose "eyes were weak." Leah represents "the affection of external truth" (AC 3758). She too is the daughter of Laban: the elder daughter. At first Jesus did not see deeply into the Word. His love for the Word was at first an *external* affection of truth or "weak-

109

eyed" which did not see the truths that could change the patterns in His not-yet-glorified natural. But this love is followed by a deeper and truer love represented by Rachel, a love of the *interior* truths of the Word. These truths lead to major changes in the Lord's life, in His natural level. In fact, they lead to His glorification of that very plane.

From the truths He learns from the Word, He begins to change in His day-to-day actions, to come into the initiation of glorification. If what is Divine comes to this natural level of life, it also opens up astonishing changes for us. It provides for us the Source for the inflowing of heavenly life. It makes it possible for us to begin to *be angels*, even here on earth.

Reuben, Simeon, Levi, and Judah, all sons of the affection of external truth (Leah), depict initial or preparatory stages that lead the way to the actual glorification of the natural. They depict a "honeymoon" state, preparing for fundamental changes to follow.

Reuben, the first-born, literally means "has seen." With Jesus, Reuben represents "foresight" (AC 3859).

"That in the supreme sense 'to see' is foresight must be evident, for the intelligence which is predicated of the Lord is infinite intelligence, which is nothing else than foresight" (AC 3863:4).

The youthful Jesus comes into Divine foresight even as He goes about His daily life in Nazareth. His reflections are of the deepest nature. He knows now not only what is happening around Him, but also what will happen in the future.

From His heredity through Mary the Lord's natural level too had been in darkness. It had lacked faith and real vision. But now a change is coming. The young Jesus is to experience an insight, a vision that initiates His natural into becoming Immanuel, God with us. His Soul, Jehovah, now unfolds before Him the inmost source of faith in the natural — Divine foresight. Here, in His natural, He begins to see with new eyes. He sees things past and future; He begins to *foresee* salvation for us, and glorification for Himself. This foresight is a glimpse into infinity, a seeing into unlimited promises and spiritual distances.

"And Leah conceived again, and bare a son, and said, 'Because Jehovah has heard that I was hated, and has given me this one also'; and she called his name Simeon" (Gen. 29:33). The Lord now works to obey His acquired faith in His daily life. This obedience is "Simeon" born within Him, replacing the finite human tendencies to ignore what His growing faith dictates for Him to do. These tendencies in His heredity through Mary, with the hells behind them, hate this obedience in Jesus. This is captured by the phrase of Leah, "I was hated" (Gen. 29:33). Simeon literally means, "to hear." With Jesus, Simeon represents the Divine Providence, because ultimately obedience to the dictates of faith expresses a full trust in this Providence. It is through Providence that the Lord hears our prayers and answers them. Providence is the source that expresses Divine hearing. With the symbolic birth of Simeon, Jesus brings the reality of Divine Providence right down into His daily life.

As the natural level of Jesus Christ came into initial states of glorification, first He foresaw the needs of humankind from eternity to eternity. Then He began to provide that a new faith should come into our natural lives. This is at the heart of His Divine Providence. He works His miracles in many ways. States of coincidence, of serendipity, come to us and help us to change our outer and inner lives. Our new faith in the natural begins to fit into our home life and our occupational life. We put truths into action.

When Simeon is born to the Lord in His glorification, it leads Him to see how He can provide for us and lead us to heaven. We are as little children in trying to perceive how this is so. This Simeon state comes to Jesus while He still lives in Nazareth, acting outwardly as a carpenter. This too is representative, for carpenters work with wood, using tools of iron. Wood corresponds to natural goodness, which is fashioned through natural truths (iron).

"And Leah conceived again, and bare a son, and said, 'Now this time will my man cleave to me, because I have borne him three sons'; therefore she called his name Levi" (Gen. 29:34). In the supreme sense, " 'to cleave' is love and mercy" (AC 3875). In the glorification of His natural, as the state of Levi comes into Jesus' heart from His Soul, He has a great longing to extend mercy to others. The Lord sees the states of all on earth and in the spiritual world at this point, and He knows the miseries of all people. He also looks ahead, into the future of humankind on earth, and knows that many hearts will suffer deep miseries. He sees the depression and feelings of being lost that will come to many. This moves Him with a powerful compassion, a Divine mercy towards human sufferers.

"And Leah conceived again, and bare a son, and she said, 'This time I will confess Jehovah'; and therefore she called his name Judah; and she stood still from bearing" (Gen. 29:35). In the supreme sense, Judah signifies the Divine of love (AC 3881). This is the love from which Divine mercy comes. It is this which the Lord now feels and perceives. That Divine of love is the goal in glorifying His natural. It will bring Divinity to this level of His mind where before had been the influence of His heredity through Mary. It is to be a transformation of inestimable spiritual impact. So far He feels this only in its beginnings.

In glorifying His natural mind, the Lord takes the Word to Himself and makes it His nature. He becomes the Word. From this He ascends toward the Divine good, toward Judah. The Divine of love (Judah) is at the top of the ladder, but there will be many more sons and rungs before the natural is fully glorified. The mother of these first four states is Leah who, as we have seen, represents an *external* affection of truth. This indicates that more beautiful and powerful states are still to follow. These are represented by Jacob's experiences in his later years in Haran as he gradually becomes wealthy and has further sons and a daughter.

For us, each of these first four sons represents a new state that can change our daily outlooks and lives. There is an initial faith in everyday life (Reuben). Then comes the desire to obey this truth (Simeon). The Lord blesses this with a sense of "charity" or love of the neighbor (Levi), followed by a new and applied love of the Lord (Judah). These are initial or "honeymoon" type states, but they bring happiness where before there was a feeling of misery.

Chapter Seventeen

LATER STAGES OF GLORIFICATION OF THE NATURAL

JACOB IN HARAN: THE LATER YEARS
GENESIS 30

+ Rachel envies her sister and gives her maid Bilhah to Jacob. Bilhah has two sons named Dan and Naphtali.

+ Leah, who had stopped having children of her own, gives her maid Zilpah to Jacob. Zilpah has two sons, Gad and Asher.

The first four sons of Jacob were all born from Leah, and represent an initial stage in the glorification of the natural of Jesus Christ. They are Divine foresight, Divine Providence, Divine mercy, and the Divine of love. These four are a "honeymoon" state, a beautiful preparatory stage leading up to the actual glorification that is now to follow.

Jacob and Rachel had a sure love for each other. They were sad that Rachel was barren. When Rachel saw that she could not bear a son, she gave Bilhah her handmaid to Jacob. Bilhah conceived and bore Jacob a son. Rachel then said: " 'God has judged me, and also has heard my voice, and has given me a son'; therefore she called his name Dan" (Gen. 30:2-6, selected).

A new series of sons is now born, and the first of these is Dan. As the firstborn in this group, he represents the key to all that follows with this unit.

In Jesus, Dan represents "justice and mercy" (AC 3920, 3923). As the young Jesus Christ comes into the actual glorification of His natural, He perceives justice and mercy as the first goals in this process, a coming into Divine justice and mercy as the foundation of the glorified Divine natural. This is not the idea of mercy represented by Levi in the first series; it is rather a mercy and justice applied to actual life needs and situations. From His Soul, He is led into the practical justice and mercy that will uplift individual human beings. In His Divine natural, the Lord begins to replace His finite inherited qualities with true justice and true mercy.

"And Bilhah conceived again, and Bilhah, Rachel's handmaid, bore a second son to Jacob. And Rachel said, 'With wrestlings of God have I wrestled with my sister, and I have prevailed'; and she called his name Naphtali" (Gen. 30:7,8). These words refer to the Lord's victories in temptations through His own power.

The Lord became incarnate to redeem and save humankind, to rescue us from the overwhelming power of the hells. To meet the hells in combat, He assumes through Mary a fallen heredity, thus giving the hells access to Himself. He meets the hells not from His Divinity within, but from His human essence. The temptations He endures are torturous, grievous beyond anything ever known. But these temptations are necessary, at this stage because they will be a means of uniting His Divine rational with His new natural. Jesus fights in these temptations from His own power, and He conquers from His own power. This is true of no one else; none of us sustains and conquers in temptations from our own power. It is the Lord Who sustains and conquers during our temptations, with a tender love for each of us.

In summary, the Lord instilled justice and mercy in His natural

(Dan) where before had been the finite heredity through Mary. He then endured further temptations (Naphtali), the real key to change and glorification. What follows is His assuming of Gad and Asher qualities.

"And Leah saw that she had stood still from bearing, and she took Zilpah her handmaid, and gave her to Jacob for a woman. And Zilpah, Leah's handmaid, bare Jacob a son. And Leah said, 'A troop comes,' and she called his name Gad" (Gen. 30:9-11). In the Lord's glorification, Gad represents omnipotence and omniscience (AC 3929). He represents that in the Lord which is all-powerful and all-knowing. After justice and mercy become a part of His natural (Dan), and Jesus then achieves victories in ongoing temptations (Naphtali), Jehovah His Soul instills a degree of the power and wisdom that will belong to Jesus' glorified natural in the end. This power and wisdom are not yet fully Divine, but He perceives the reality of omnipotence and omniscience and that they will become His with the completion of the glorification process.

With the quality represented by Gad, when it is born to Jesus' natural level, there comes a sense of power from Divine love, and awareness and knowing from Divine intelligence. In His natural level there is a dawning awareness of infinite power and intelligence.

An increasing sense of Divinity is coming to Jesus. Its very source is the Divine Love in His Soul. This power, this intelligence, will serve to save humankind from destruction by the hells. It will also save us in moments of overwhelming need. There are times when we are about to be overwhelmed by some evil, and the touch of Providence rescues us. This is the Lord's touch from His now glorified Divine Human. He redeems us.

The omnipotence and omniscience in God are far beyond our grasp or perception. But they inflow from the Lord, through His Divine Human, accommodated to our daily lives. They inflow through the operation of His Holy Spirit, which is His Divine

Human touching and uplifting our hearts and minds. For Jesus Christ on earth, His coming into the representation of Gad is a major step in enabling Him to assist us. The all-powerful and all-knowing Divine, represented by Gad, inflows especially into useful services that we perform for others.

Another quality is represented by the birth of Asher. **"And Zilpah, Leah's handmaid, bare a second son to Jacob. And Leah said, 'In my blessedness, for the daughters will call me blessed'; and she called his name Asher" (Gen. 30:12, 13).** In the Lord's glorification, Asher represents *"eternity,* [and] in the internal sense the happiness of eternal life. . . ." (AC 3936, emphasis added).

Eternal life becomes completely real to Jesus in His natural, and He sees that the eternal or eternity is to become His very nature when He and the Father become One. This will be a source of awe and joy.

If we think of eternity as being *in the Lord* and in His accommodated but pure love, it becomes a source of happiness and of a sense of reality and hope. With angels, each state the Lord gives to them is sparklingly alive. They always live in the present with openness and delight.

So we read that such angels are not worried or anxious about the future, and if we are striving to become angels, we must strive for this state as well:

"Unruffled is their spirit whether they obtain the objects of their desire or not; and they do not grieve over the loss of them, being content with their lot. If they become rich, they do not set their hearts on riches; if they are raised to honors, they do not regard themselves as more worthy than others; if they become poor, they are not made sad; if their circumstances are mean, they are not dejected. They know that for those who trust in the Divine, all things advance toward a happy state to eternity, and that whatever befalls them in time is still conducive thereto.

Be it known that the Divine Providence is universal, that is, in things the most minute; and that they who are in the stream of Providence are all the time carried along toward everything that is happy, whatever may be the appearance of the means; and that those are in the stream of Providence who put their trust in the Divine, and attribute all things to Him. . . .Be it known also that so far as anyone is in the stream of Providence, so far he is in a state of peace" (AC 8478:3,4).

Chapter Eighteen

FURTHER STAGES OF GLORIFICATION OF THE NATURAL

THE BIRTHS OF ISSACHAR, ZEBULUN, AND DINAH
GENESIS 30 CONTINUED

+ **Leah conceives again and bears sons named Issachar and Zebulun and a daughter named Dinah.**

"And Reuben went in the days of the wheat-harvest, and found dudaim in the field, and brought them unto Leah his mother" (Gen. 30:14). Rachel asked for these dudaim, and Leah agreed to give them to her in exchange for Jacob's cohabiting with Leah that night. The "dudaim" represent the "things of conjugial love in the truth and good of charity and love" (AC 3942).

"What the 'dudaim' were, the translators do not know. They suppose them to have been fruits or flowers, to which they give names according to their several opinions. But of what kind they were it does not concern us to know. . . .By the 'dudaim' there is signified the conjugial of good and truth. . . .It is derived from the word 'dudim,' which means loves and conjunction by means of them" (*Ibid.*).

The focus is now on the final key stages of the glorification of the Lord's natural. The subject is a progressive conjunction of Divine good and Divine truth. From these come the influx and force enabling good and truth (love and faith) progressively to unite in us. And this uniting brings us into heaven even on our natural level.

In the literal story, the two wives of Jacob have an exchange. Leah, the wife less loved by Jacob, agrees to give up her dudaim to Rachel only if she may join with their husband that night. There is a longing expressed by both women in this incident. Rachel, who already possesses the greater love from Jacob, longs for the dudaim. Leah longs for closeness with Jacob, and to conceive more children by him. Each wife agrees to give to the other what she desires.

Jacob represents the natural-level delight that Jesus feels in response to true ideas. An affection for deeper, interior truth (Rachel) is more precious and beautiful to Him than an affection for outer, external truth (Leah). And yet a joining of natural delight with outer, natural-world truth must come first in order for Jesus to make His natural mind Divine. Leah's children must be born before Rachel's. In His natural mind, Jesus must embrace the truths in the knowledge of nature and the literal sense of the Word with delight, because these too ultimately come from the Divine.

One might wonder why Jesus could not move directly into conjunction with interior truth. Why did He take this step, first to join His natural-level delight with external truth? Because this is the route that we, as finite humans, must take. Without a foundation of delight in outer truth, we would have no ability to move into deeper, spiritual knowledge with equal delight. When we first learn to delight in the warmth of the sun, we lay a foundation that can lead to a delight in the knowledge of God's love, which is represented by the sun's warmth. In order to bring Divinity to the path we must take, Jesus chooses to develop His mind in this order. His maternal heredity also leads to this pathway.

Just as both wives gain something in this exchange in Genesis 30, both levels of affection in Jesus gain something through this process. **In the literal story, Leah gains conjunction with her husband, and then bears two more sons and a daughter. Rachel gains the dudaim,** which represent the "things of conjugial love." These representations symbolize a joining of Jesus' natural-level delight with outer truth (Jacob and Leah), which then brings about a deeper joining that can take place (Jacob and Rachel). He is now able to move into the "heavenly marriage" of delight in His natural consciousness with deeper, interior truth and principles. The two last sons and the daughter that are born to Jacob and Leah prepare the way for the deeper conjunction, the heavenly marriage, which in the literal story will finally bring a child to Jacob and Rachel.

Regeneration or rebirth comes from the heavenly marriage of good and truth in the human mind. Truth longs for good, which is its interior partner, and good needs truths to clothe its love. In other words, faith needs to feel love for what it knows to be true, and love needs knowledge to bring it into life. On the highest level, coming from the soul itself, a conjugial or marriage principle is now at work. This is an interior force or influx into the mind working towards a heavenly marriage. From this marriage, a person becomes an angel. What are truths alone except statements? What are goods or loves without definition, which truth provides? Good or love is the heart, but it needs its clothing of truths to have any effect or use.

Jacob came to Leah that night, and "he lay with her" (Gen. 30:16). From this came the conception and birth of Issachar, the ninth of Jacob's twelve sons. In speaking of the heavenly marriage now taking place, the Writings reveal a new principle: that this marriage is between the good of a lower plane and the truth of a higher one (AC 3952). Lower goods need the discipline of truths from a higher level of revelation. For example, the good of a sexual relationship needs the higher truths regarding conjugial love, or the outer sexual act will be profaned. With the Lord, the marriage is between His Divine Human and the Divine itself, His Soul. This is a holy marriage between the Son of God (His Divine Human) and the Father. In the Lord these two became One by glorification (see AC 3952:2). "I and My Father are One" (John 10:30).

The first birth in this new series is that of Issachar, son of Leah and Jacob. When this fifth son of Jacob and Leah was born, Leah said: " 'God has given me my reward, because I gave my handmaid to my man.' And she called his name Issachar" (Gen. 30:18).

On the human plane, in the rebirth of the natural level, Issachar represents mutual love. This is a "reward" in human life that is discretely above any natural definition of reward. In fact, the very concept of reward is left behind and replaced by mutual love, a real love of others and their happiness, which is returned. Such a love is heavenly in us and can come from the Lord alone. This explains why, in the supreme sense, Issachar represents Divine good and Divine truth in Jesus Christ Himself. Divine good expresses a Divine love for others, and this has its own inmost Divine truths. These now come as new qualities in His natural.

On His plane of glorification, the Lord comes into a new, fuller love of humankind. From this He inflows into believers, endowing them with mutual love. This is a crucial step in His glorification.

"And Leah conceived again, and bare a sixth son to Jacob. And Leah said, 'God has endowed me with a good dowry; now will my man dwell with me, because I have borne him six sons'; and she called his name Zebulun" (Gen. 30:19,20). In the supreme sense, these words signify *"the Divine itself of the Lord and His Divine Human*; in the internal sense, the heavenly marriage, and in the external sense, conjugial love" (AC 3958, emphasis added).

In the supreme sense, dealing with the Lord's glorification, the coming of Zebulun is of profound significance. It signifies the

"One-ness" Who is Jesus Christ (AC 3960:3), Jesus being the Divine Love, and Christ the Divine Wisdom. These are not two but One (AC 3960:1). With the birth of Zebulun in the glorification, Jesus Christ on earth comes into a new and very special state. He enters into the beginning of the Divine Marriage. From this Divine Marriage within Himself comes the heavenly marriage in our inner minds and the conjugial promise in our everyday lives. Since the conjugial is the first source of all our happiness (CL 64), this birth is a coming of the Prince of Peace. With the Lord in His glorification, it is a new sense of Oneness with the Father, and a joy exceeding all joys (AC 2034). It is an early stage of Divine union, and it prophesies all the stages to follow.

"And afterwards she bare a daughter, and called her name Dinah" (Gen. 30:21). Dinah represents a new affection born to Jesus for all the general truths symbolized by the ten sons of Jacob by Leah and the handmaids (AC 3963). Now, finally, the way is prepared for a birth from the "heavenly marriage" between Jacob and Rachel. A love for deep, interior truth can conjoin with good in the natural consciousness of Jesus.

Chapter Nineteen

ADVANCED GLORIFICATION OF THE NATURAL

JOSEPH BORN, JACOB ENRICHED
GENESIS 30 CONTINUED

- ✦ Rachel finally conceives and has a son named Joseph.
- ✦ Jacob decides it is time to leave Laban, but Laban doesn't want him to go because he has prospered with Jacob working for him. Jacob agrees to stay on longer if he is allowed to keep the speckled and spotted goats and black lambs from Laban's herds.
- ✦ Jacob shrewdly builds up large flocks of the healthiest goats and lambs.

"And God remembered Rachel, and God hearkened to her, and opened her womb. And she conceived, and bare a son, and said, 'God has gathered my reproach.' And she called his name Joseph, saying, 'Let Jehovah add to me another son' " (Gen. 30:22-24). With Joseph's birth a new era begins, a new stage in the glorification and the coming of a new love in Jesus. Joseph's birth is like the morning star.

Joseph's life story in Genesis – his dreams, his betrayal, his exile in Egypt, and then his coming to great power – indicates his high representation. Swedenborg's Writings say that here in Genesis Joseph represents "the celestial-spiritual man" (AC 3969: 3). The celestial level is love, and its inmost is love of the Lord. With the Lord Jesus Christ on earth, the birth of Joseph heralds the coming completion of the glorification. For "Joseph" with Him is a celestial quality in His inner level. That is, Jesus Christ on earth comes into a love of His Soul, Jehovah, that He has not before experienced.

This new love leads Him to hunger for union with the Divine Love that is behind all creation. It looks to the Easter resurrection, to the complete Divine marriage, which brings into reality the glorified Lord Jesus Christ, the one God of heaven and earth. The Father and Son will then truly be One.

So far Joseph is only a newborn babe. He is fragile and dependent on his parents, Jacob and Rachel. But he is present and heralds changes that are to come. **The Genesis story still focuses on Jacob, his relationship to Laban, and finally on his return to Canaan.** This indicates that the glorification of the natural is still the major theme. But in the process a new love has been born.

Now the love that the Lord always wanted, an unimpeded love for Jehovah, has come to Him. He feels alive on both the spiritual and natural levels, whereas the finite maternal heredity had blocked the way before. This enables Him to be present with us as He never has been before. Yet this is only the beginning of this miracle.

In our own rebirth process Joseph's birth is also a miracle. Joseph is the birth of a celestial love that leads to wise innocence — a wisdom that is willing to be led by the Lord.

Joseph's birth means much to Jesus. The Word speaks of this in Jacob's later blessing of this son:

"Joseph is the son of a fruitful one, the son of a fruitful one by a fountain. . . .He shall abide in the strength of his bow; and the arms of his hands shall be made strong by the hands of the

Mighty One of Jacob; from there is the Shepherd, the Stone of Israel, by the God of your father, and He shall help you, and with Shaddai, and He shall bless you with blessings of heaven above, with blessings of the deep that lies beneath, blessings of the breasts and of the womb; the blessings of your father shall prevail over the blessings of my progenitors even to the desire of the everlasting hills; they shall be upon the head of Joseph. . ." (Gen. 49:22-26).

Much of this Divine, poetic blessing is mysterious, but its affectional and poetic ring is clear: Joseph brings wondrous blessings which reach to "the everlasting hills." He is the Shepherd and the Stone of Israel.

"And it came to pass, when Rachel had borne Joseph, that Jacob said unto Laban, 'Send me away, and I will go to my place, and to my land. Give me my females, and my children, for whom I have served you, and I will go; for you know my service wherewith I have served you'" (Gen. 30: 25, 26).

As soon as Joseph is born, there is a very significant change of state in the Lord's glorification. A celestial-spiritual love is born and inflows into the corresponding order in the natural level of the mind. This love is a powerful combination of a celestial love of Jehovah with a spiritual love of all humankind. With this there is an uplifting, a sense of exhilaration. This is just the beginning of this influx, but it makes an immediate difference.

Therefore, immediately after Joseph was born, **Jacob said to Laban, "Send me away, and I will go to my place, and to my land"** (Gen. 30:25). Jacob, goodness of truth in the natural level, now wants to dissociate from the mediate good represented by Laban. He begins to be uncomfortable in Laban's presence. Higher goods and truths have now come into the Lord's natural level, and the Jacob within desires to get away from the self-serving qualities Laban now represents. Representations in the stories of the Word change within general parameters, according to the spiritual context, and Laban at this point represents the lower of evil qualities in mediate good. In the context of a prior chapter Laban represented remains, but remains with flaws attached to them.

Jacob longed to get back home to his parents, to Isaac and Rebekah. "There was a longing of the natural represented by Jacob for a state of conjunction with the Divine of the rational" (AC 3973), represented by Isaac and Rebekah (*Ibid.*).

But Laban realized how much he had been blessed by Jacob's service, how much he had been enriched. So he now earnestly requested Jacob to stay, and asked what reward he could offer if he would stay. Jacob replied that he would stay if he were permitted to pass through all Laban's "flocks today, removing from them every small cattle, and goats that are speckled and spotted, and every black one among the lambs, and these shall be my reward" (Gen. 30:32). Laban agreed, and Jacob proceeded to procure this reward. He also increased the offspring of these selected types by a technique that stimulated their procreation.

What is all this about in the internal sense? Certainly it would not be a part of the Lord's Word if it were only about Jacob's flocks being increased! But within, it speaks about a miracle of the Lord's government. It speaks of mediate good, and of the way that by means of goods that are lower and not genuine, the Lord can lead us into goods and truths that *are* genuine. For example, merit is a mediate good. With little children and young adults, a sense of merit is needed and can lead in time to higher goods that are free from merit. For a long time merit has innocence within it, and it is permitted, in Providence, to be a stepping-stone leading to higher goods. Therefore, this merit is a mixture of something good and something wrong, just as the flocks that Jacob selected had on them a mixture of darkness and light.

But what were the mediate goods with the Lord Himself?

Because of His spiritual-celestial endowment at birth and His Divine Soul, His mediate goods would have been of a higher nature. For instance, He fought against merit in temptations in very early childhood and overcame merit in that state (see the AC treatment of Gen. 14). Because of His Mary heredity there would have been mediate good states in the Lord. He was not born regenerate. The nature of the specific mediate goods with Jesus Christ on earth is not revealed. We are told that these had "what is human" within them (AC 4026). And it is revealed that in Him and by Him there was an absolute separation of the goods signified by "Laban" from the higher or pure goods (AC 4026).

Chapter Twenty

FURTHER GLORIFICATION

JACOB SEPARATES FROM LABAN
GENESIS 31

- ✦ Laban and his sons become openly jealous and angry with Jacob.
- ✦ Jehovah appears to Jacob and tells him to return to Canaan. Jacob and his family flee from Laban with the possessions Jacob had earned.
- ✦ Laban and his sons pursue Jacob and catch up with Jacob and his family.
- ✦ Laban and Jacob argue over whether Jacob should be allowed to leave with Laban's daughters and the possessions Jacob has earned.
- ✦ Jacob and Laban settle their dispute and make a covenant to stay out of each other's territory.

Jacob had served Laban for twenty years, fourteen years for his two daughters and six years for his flocks. He found Laban a harsh father-in-law. Although the farmstead had been blessed under Jacob's leadership, it was also true that Jacob had been greatly enriched himself. Laban's sons saw this, and unfairly criticized Jacob: "Jacob has taken all that was our father's, and from that which was our father's has he made all this abundance" (Gen. 31:1).

"And Jacob saw the faces of Laban, and behold, he was not at all with him, as yesterday and the day before. And Jehovah said unto Jacob, 'Return unto the land of your fathers, and to your nativity, and I will be with you' " (Gen. 31:2,3). "Faces" represent interior qualities (AC 4066); the plural is used because of the many different qualities that compose mediate good or Laban. Laban and Jacob had both changed in the years that Jacob spent in Paddan-aram. Representatively, Jacob had become more caring, mellower, and less personally ambitious, whereas Laban had gradually hardened and become more and more distant from his son-in-law.

The time had come for them to separate. Mediate good is a means to an end. The end is the establishment of genuine goods and truths in the natural mind. **These are Jacob's flocks and also his wives and children.** Since mediate good has selfishness at its core, it must eventually be left behind; we can no longer operate from mixed motives. This change is what is now happening. **Jehovah Himself is calling Jacob to leave Laban and return to the land of Canaan.** This is reminiscent of Abram's being called in far earlier days to leave Haran and travel to the land of Canaan. But Abram was to establish a home in the Holy Land, **whereas Jacob was returning home to the place of his "fathers, and to (his). . .nativity"** (Gen. 32:3).

Jacob conferred with Leah and Rachel about his call to return home and his desire to leave Laban, who had been such a cruel taskmaster. His wives agreed with him, and so they gathered up their families and possessions and left without Laban's knowledge. Also, Rachel stole her father's idols or teraphim (Gen. 31:9).

When news reached Laban that Jacob and his family had

departed, Laban gathered his men and pursued in anger. He felt that all of Jacob's goods and family were his own, although they were not. Laban might well have attacked Jacob and perhaps even killed him, but "God came to Laban the Aramean in a dream by night, and said unto him, 'Take heed to yourself lest you speak with Jacob from good even to evil' " (Gen. 31:24). It was a warning from God to leave Jacob untouched.

Jacob and Laban met in the mountains of Gilead, and each made harsh accusations against the other. After much arguing, Laban finally came into a wholly different state, one of reconciliation. Laban and Jacob made a covenant and separated in peace (Gen. 31:48-55).

The Laban-Jacob story tells how the Lord "made His natural Divine" (AC 4065). He used mediate goods as a means to procure those things needed for the glorification of His natural. He did this by "His own power" (*Ibid.*), unlike ourselves. We might think that the Lord would not employ mediate goods. But the Word responds: "The Divine Itself has need of none, not even of that mediate good, except that He willed that all things should be done according to order" (*Ibid.*). He took this path so that we would have a path to follow.

Jacob was told by Jehovah to "return to the land of your fathers" (Gen. 31:3). This verse means that Jesus (as Jacob) should now "betake Himself nearer to good Divine" (AC 4069). **Jacob should return and go to Isaac.** The glorification of the Lord's natural is nearing completion, and He is ready to become one with Isaac, the Divine rational (AC 4069).

The Writings of Swedenborg teach much about our connection with people in the spiritual world. They describe how our spirits actually travel from place to place in the spiritual world as we grow and change. With each new development, we associate ourselves with a new "society" or group of spirits or angels.

Jesus "summoned to Himself such [heavenly societies] as

might be of service, and changed them at His good pleasure" (AC 4075). He did this in order that by means of them He might glorify His natural and thus be able to redeem and save us. He in no way harmed these societies but rather by means of them acquired *Divine* goods and truths that would help everyone. At the same time, by having this process involve so many societies, He put both heaven and hell into order (*Ibid.*). We may forget this vital aspect of the Lord's work on earth: part of His redeeming or rescuing us lay in His bringing order back to the spiritual world. He did this partly through this process, but also more powerfully through temptations and victories. He ordered the heavens, and subjugated and ordered the hells. Thereby He redeemed us.

Jesus Christ on earth, living in Nazareth as a young man, is doing work of eternal importance in His spirit. Within Himself, having an overview of all things in creation, He successively draws to Himself certain spiritual societies in an intricate and beautiful pattern, and by means of this He learns ever more interior things. At the same time, He orders these societies in new ways, removing evils that obstruct, ordering goods where needed. He is the Redeemer. This Man, while in His body in Nazareth, is the Divine rescuer. He is ordering and healing spiritual societies, and at the same time glorifying His own natural. This is possible because of His Soul and His endowments.

He sees what merit is like from societies who take merit, and then leads Himself to see the goodness of taking no merit at all, which is a state from the Divine (AC 4065).

He sees societies of spirits who love to reason about goods and truths, and who think themselves very wise. Studying these societies, He perceives that they are in mental shade, and that without Divine mercy regarding their states they will spiritually perish (AC 4075: 2). He observes societies that *say* they are in love to God, but look only to the vast Infinite and worship an invisible God. He sees that unless they have some finite concept of God they will be "looking into thick darkness" only (AC 4075:3) and will have only strange and false fancies. He sees the terribly limited nature of their ideas and realizes their need to have a visible Divine Human to see and worship.

All these things He learns as He processes these spiritual societies. He gains knowledge by means of them, but not directly from them. He learns by means of His own Laban states, but receives no qualities *from* them. Rather, the states that become His own are Divine.

The Lord in His glorification now turns to a new goal. This is pictured in **Jacob's leaving Paddan-aram, "to go to Isaac his father in the land of Canaan" (Gen. 31:18).** As His natural is glorified, the Lord looks to uniting His natural level with His Divine rational, which is Isaac. He looks to becoming integrated, Divine on both planes, and alive in a way that He has not been before: alive as the only true Human, One with His Soul. But still He needs to take steps before His natural is ready for such advanced glorification. **Jacob has to cross into the borderlands of Canaan, meet an angel there, and then be reconciled with Esau, whom he fears.**

A major step in this direction of reuniting with Isaac comes when Jacob and his family and flocks crosses over the Euphrates, which is the extreme boundary of the land of Canaan in its widest sense. Crossing this boundary is a coming into a "conjunction. . . with the Divine" (AC 4116). It is not the complete conjunction and integration, but a vital step in this direction, and a step away from Laban's homeland.

Chapter Twenty-One

THE LORD'S TEMPTATIONS IN GLORIFYING HIS NATURAL

COMING HOME
GENESIS 32

✦ On his way back to Canaan Jacob sends out
  messengers to Esau, his brother. The messengers
  return, saying Esau is coming toward him with
  four hundred men.

✦ Jacob is afraid and separates his family into groups to
  allow for an escape if Esau attacks.

✦ During the night Jacob wrestles with an angel
  and prevails. Jacob is then renamed Israel by God.

After twenty years away from his parents and his homeland
of Canaan, Jacob now journeyed toward a reunion. For him the
most feared aspect of this return was his meeting with Esau.
Before leaving Canaan many years earlier, Jacob had twice
betrayed his older brother. Esau had sworn revenge at that
time; in fact he had intended to kill Jacob. Jacob's fear on
returning seemed justified. But twenty years *had* gone by, and
in such a long time many changes occur.

After Jacob and his family separated from Laban and went
on their way, the Word says, "the angels of God ran to meet

him" (Gen. 32:1). Again, the angels! First in his dream of the ladder at Bethel and now, two decades later, as Jacob came near home. The "angels" are enlightenment coming in from goodness, preparing us for the meeting with Esau, preparing Jacob within us to meet the older brother. It is a readying for truth to come to inner good and to discover that goodness is the ruler of the heart. If we have been living the truth in many, many states, this upcoming change frightens us. It will alter our patterns. We will lose our former moorings. We are afraid we will lose everything, emotionally and spiritually. So the Lord sends His angels to give us inner warmth and light and to guide us home.

The Lord brings about this change in us with Divine wisdom and gentleness. He has established on His own plane on earth the same process (AC 4234). The Isaac level of the Lord has been glorified. But the natural level, represented by Jacob and Esau, is only in the process of glorification. On this plane there had been strong tendencies to evil through the finite human nature inherited through Mary. Jesus Christ started out with Jacob leading the way: He compelled His hereditary natural to obey Divine truth. He is now ready to go on His way to Esau: to experience a reunion with Esau that brings Divinity to His very natural (AC 4234). When Jesus comes to love the principles of Divine Truth in His natural-level consciousness, self-compulsion is no longer necessary. True principles meet with love and delight, and then living them is pure joy.

These changes within the Lord will have direct impact on our natural emotions and ideals, on our ordinary thoughts and day-to-day life.

When Jacob and Esau are united in Jesus Christ and His natural is glorified, He comes to us in a new way. It is like the returning of someone we love deeply who has been far away but now comes home, enters our door, and takes us into his arms. By coming home he gives us a warmth and light we would never know without him (TCR 109). One of Jesus' greatest gifts is that He glorifies His natural level, and that He puts Esau or Divine good first, with Jacob becoming as one who serves. Good comes first with Him — the strong and wonderful good of the love of others, and this in His very Natural (TCR 43). We pray that someday it may be so with us.

The process by which truth acknowledges good to be superior, to be the heart of life, is seen in harmonious detail in the coming together of Jacob and Esau. **Jacob sent messengers ahead to Esau and said to them, "Thus shall you say to my lord Esau" (Gen. 32:4), and through them Jacob relays to Esau his experience in Haran.** The words **"My lord Esau"** signify "the first acknowledgment of good as being in the higher place" (AC 4242). Jacob did not call Esau his brother, but his "lord," and also later he calls himself Esau's "servant" (*Ibid.*). This is drawing near the "inversion" (AC 4243) in which good will come to lead the way. This is what was hoped for in the beginning, and now, after successive steps of rebirth, it is actually happening.

When they had talked with Esau and returned, the messengers of Jacob said, "We came to your brother, to Esau, and moreover he comes to meet you, and four hundred men with him" (Gen. 32:6). Good is now coming to the truth within Jesus. This good brings "four hundred men" with it! This struck fear into Jacob. His brother was coming, and Jacob feared it was to take vengeance for his misdeeds twenty years earlier. Jacob's outward fear speaks spiritually of an inward anxiety that comes with temptation. "Four hundred" represents temptation.

Jesus on earth, while in Nazareth, goes through these inner clouds and storms. **"And Jacob remained alone, and there wrestled a man with him until the dawn arose."** Here it is the Lord's temptation in glorifying His natural that is the subject. He undergoes a most grievous temptation, so grievous that He wrestles not only with the hells, but also *with the angels*: "That the Lord in temptation at last fought with the angels themselves, no, with the whole angelic heaven, is a secret that has not yet been disclosed"

(AC 4295:2).

When the hells attack Jesus through the maternal human, the issue is saving humankind. They focus on how evil humankind is, and instill despair over His purpose of saving us. This is a powerful trial, for the hells have much of lower realities on their side. They try to deflect the Lord from the higher reality that many human beings choose heaven in freedom!

But how do the angels tempt Him? Angels are the most loving and caring people in all creation. Why would the Lord combat them? It is vital to see that He would never have had to fight against the genuine wisdom and love within them. These only want to serve the Lord and others. Ordinarily, the angels are in elevated or morning and noon states of mind, when their love for the Lord and others is full of joy and life.

But in twilight states of mind, their hereditary evils are nearer. At the time of the Lord's life on earth and His temptations, the spiritual world had great disorders, such as imaginary heavens, ruled by evil genii. Devils had infiltrated the borders of heaven itself, and disorder and confusion existed there from such an evil presence. When the Lord endures temptations from the angels and conquers their illusions, He brings the heavens back into order. He restores the heavens to the full beauty of the human form, or Grand Man. Before this, the heavens are strongly disturbed. Terrible fears for the salvation of human beings on earth overwhelm them.

The angels love the Lord deeply, with all their "hearts, souls, minds and strength" (Mark 12:30). Do they not want to relieve the Lord of His almost unbearable torment? Wouldn't they perceive the part-truth that the hells were insinuating into Him: that humankind is too evil to be saved? Given these things, perhaps the angels focused on the Lord's chief end: to save us. They perceived how in myriad cases this seems almost impossible.

The angels then, in a state of obscurity, try to instill in Jesus an immediate apparent need: to force humankind into goodness. The most powerful evil, the love of dominion, would work through the angels' low states and urge the Lord to "command that these stones become bread" (Matt. 4:3). The angels would urge this innocently, out of misguided love, and in agonized obscurity.

If this is the case, angels have temporarily lost faith in humankind. They are wrong. Nothing is more precious than leaving human beings in final freedom to choose heaven or hell with no over-ruling compulsion. That it is the angels who tempt Him is terribly hard for Jesus, Who is love itself.

Jesus Christ must at times feel quite alone except for the beauty of His Divine Soul, which in temptation seems remote. Yet He does not yield to the angels. He endures a terrible torment and struggles even to near despair. But then love triumphs; He wrestles and wins. He does this in order to preserve that very essential of our humanity: our spiritual freedom.

The Lord leads the angels back to basic truths and goods, and then restores the heavens to true order. The temptations from them cease. **The "sun arose to Jacob" (Gen. 32:31). Jacob and the angel ceased wrestling. Peace came, and a blessing.**

The angel changed Jacob's name to "Israel" — the angel who now represents the Divine inflowing. **This new name marks a major change in Jacob's life.** Names signify qualities, and after the victory in this temptation, Jesus in His natural comes into a new quality (AC 4286). Now celestial good inflows through truth into the natural level of the Lord as it had not done before. He therefore has a new name: "Israel." This is celestial love come into His natural life.

Each major temptation of Jesus Christ, as revealed in the *Arcana*, focuses on His love for the salvation of humankind. In childhood He fights and conquers those hells that stand between Him and an innocent love of salvation (Gen. 14). As a young man, He fights for the preservation of the Divine rational in its vulnerable beginnings (Gen. 22, the near sacrifice of Isaac), for this rational is the vital tool in saving us. Now, in wrestling and overcoming the angel, Israel is established. The Divine natural is firmly in place and needs only a few further steps for its complete glorification. This Divine natural makes our regeneration possible.

This change in the Lord opens the way for His reunion with Esau, the Divine good in His natural, which is eternally optimistic about humankind, and in this is Divinely realistic.

As Esau and Jacob meet, and Esau becomes the leader, so the Lord leads us to a realization that the whole purpose in the rebirth of the natural in Himself — and in us — is that Divine good may come into the human heart. He is our Father, Who took the path first, and now tenderly and lovingly invites us to follow Him, to take the journey to heaven, even while He holds our hand.

Chapter Twenty-Two

GLORIFICATION OF THE NATURAL NEARS COMPLETION

THE RECONCILIATION OF JACOB AND ESAU
GENESIS 33

+ Jacob fearfully approaches Esau, but Esau runs to embrace him and they are happily reunited.

+ Jacob convinces Esau to return to where he came from, and Jacob and his family travel slowly to Succoth and buy land there.

"And Jacob lifted up his eyes, and saw, and behold, Esau came, and with him four hundred men. And Jacob divided the children over unto Leah, and over unto Rachel, and over unto the two handmaids. And he put the handmaids and their children first, and Leah and her children after, and Rachel and Joseph after. And he himself passed over before them, and bowed himself to the earth seven times, until he drew near unto his brother. And Esau ran to meet him, and embraced him, and fell upon his neck, and kissed him, and they wept" (Gen. 33:1-4).

At last the twin brothers were reunited. Jacob had approached Esau with fear. Esau had come to him with four hundred warriors. But there was no anger, no confrontation.

Instead, Esau ran to Jacob and embraced him with great love. The two wept together, not in sorrow but in relief and joy. This marks another new state in the Lord's glorification on earth. Divine good can now at last rule in the natural with the fullness of love. Where before there had been self-compulsion and temptation, Divine love has now come to bring glorification. Jesus is still in Nazareth, a young adult in appearance, doing the work of a carpenter. But within He is the Divine carpenter of glorification and rebirth.

This stage of the glorification of the natural level of the Lord is the key to our own rebirth. Temptations and victories effect such rebirth with us. The reunion of Esau and Jacob came only by Jacob's undergoing fear and anxiety and at last coming into submission and genuine humility (see AC 4341:2). The limited truth with us becomes anxious when good itself approaches, and it undergoes temptations and profound revisions. These in turn lead to reconciliation, reunion, and release. The goal of Esau as leader is achieved, not with bitterness or outward friction, but with love from the very heart. On this natural plane we are free.

With Jesus, this reunion is the reunion of Divine good and truth, and His joy relates not only to Himself, but also and especially to the meaning of this union in Himself for humankind. He knows what it will mean to us. At last we are able to be in a harmony with Him, and by our free choice. This reunion brings the Lord surpassing joy, for it is a fulfillment of His love.

When Jacob was reconciled with Esau, he said, "I have seen your faces like seeing the faces of God, and you have accepted me" (Gen. 33:10). This is the truth in our natural level seeing goodness at last, goodness like "the faces of God." When this really happens to us, when we see it in our natural lives, it stirs the affections and brings an inner love of others, a love made real by performing useful services, especially spiritual services, for others.

This state of experiencing love of others in our natural level deepens step by step. The full uniting of Jacob and Esau, on the spiritual plane, is successive, stage by stage (see AC 4375 *et al*). In each increasing stage of closeness we experience greater delight, usefulness, and creativity.

Jacob now traveled on with his family and possessions to Shalem, a city of Shechem. Shalem "means tranquility and perfection" (AC 4393). This is so with the Lord on earth. With the union of Good and Truth in Him, as it progresses step by step, there comes increasing tranquility. After a few more stages, the natural with Him is glorified. In this, with Him, is "perfection."

Here in Shalem Jacob raised an altar to worship Jehovah, to thank Him for his safe return home and his reunion with Esau. He called the altar "El Elohe Israel," which means "God of gods" (AC 4402:4). Jesus Christ has now come to a stage in His glorification where Divine truths joined with Divine goods have become a part of Himself in His natural. In the Isaiah prophecy, this indicates an attainment of the next successive stage of the glorification: "And His name will be called Wonderful, Counselor, *God, Hero*" (Isaiah 9:6, emphasis added). He has not become "*God*" on this plane without also being a "*Hero*," that is, a victor in most grievous temptations.

Ahead are increasing heights of glorification and even greater struggles against the hells. Beyond those He will become "the Father of Eternity, and the Prince of Peace" (Isaiah 9:6). He will achieve this as He turns to the glorification of His sensuous level and finally of His very body.

Chapter Twenty-Three

THE FALLEN SENSUOUS

THE LOST DREAM
GENESIS 34

✦ Shechem, a prince of the country, rapes Jacob's
   daughter Dinah.

✦ Yet Shechem loves Dinah, and his father asks
   Jacob and her brothers if Shechem may marry her.

✦ Dinah's brothers say they will allow the marriage
   if the males of the land will be circumcised. In
   reality, they have no intention of allowing it at all.

✦ Shechem and his father consent, and when they are
   recovering from the circumcisions, Simeon and Levi,
   Dinah's brothers, kill them, and all the sons plunder
   the city.

✦ Jacob rebukes Simeon and Levi.

Chapter 34 in the Genesis narrative tells of the rape of
Dinah by Shechem and the dreadful revenge of her brothers.
This is the sad story of a forced sexual union followed by an
extreme and evil revenge. What has this to do with the Lord's
glorification? Why is it placed spiritually or representatively in

the context of late stages of the glorification of the Lord's natural?

This story appears where it does because this is where it belongs. It tells of evils that may possibly overwhelm the sensuous, that is, the level of the senses in human beings. Coming soon is Jesus' confrontation of these sensuous evils and His battle with them in His glorification process.

People who had descended from the members of the *Most Ancient Church*, the first church on earth with the earliest peoples on earth, still existed in the land of Canaan at the time of Jacob and his children, "especially among those called the Hittites and Hivites" (AC 4447:2,3). What kind of a people were they? It may be said that Hamor and Shechem were of the last peoples of a Golden Age, and that in a sense this chapter re-enacts the fall of that Golden Age and repeats it perhaps for the final time.

But it was Shechem who forced Dinah. From his point of view this union turned out to be more than only sexual, for he genuinely wanted her in marriage. This desire of Shechem to join with Dinah represents the Hivites' desire to join with Jacob's clan. The outer rites that Jacob and his family practiced were familiar to the Hivites. These rites represented deeper principles that ancient religions, ancestors of the Hivites, had lived by. Thus Shechem and his tribe were drawn to Dinah and her family (AC 4449). **Hamor, Shechem's father, endeavored to arrange a marriage. To achieve this goal, Hamor and Shechem agreed to be circumcised in order to be acceptable to the Jews.** In speaking of their agreeing to circumcision, the Lord reveals in Swedenborg's Writings that "Hamor and Shechem his son committed an enormous sin in receiving circumcision" (AC 4489:4e).

This was because, as people of the Most Ancient Church, Hamor and Shechem were internal in nature (AC 4489:3). But circumcision is an external rite, symbolic for the representative of a church, the Israelitish Church, which rejected internal things. In accepting circumcision, Hamor and Shechem and their followers turned away from celestial things to empty externals, from a celestial innocence to a sensuous act.

The sons of Jacob had no desire to join with deeper principles of religion. They were content with mere external rites. Therefore, the only way that the Hivites could join their ancient religion with this new one would be by forcing the union (AC 4433), and this is represented by the fact that Shechem forced himself on Dinah.

A marriage between Shechem and Dinah would have been a good union, representing a union between external rites and deeper religious principles of the heart and mind. This could have re-established the wisdom of the Ancient Church with the sons of Jacob (AC 4439). Yet no union can become real if it is forced. Though Shechem's desire was a good one, his method was very wrong. There could be no union here, because the children of Jacob did not want one.

Here the fall of the Most Ancient Church is re-enacted in a nearly final incident in the history of this Hivite clan, for it led to their complete extermination by the murderous swords of Simeon and Levi. Externally we find much that is brutal and coarse in this story. Internally it speaks of gentle and innocent love being lost. When innocence is truly lost, its loss is sad beyond anything else that can happen.

Because of their fall from innocence, the Lord permitted the Hivites in this Hamor/Shechem clan to be entirely destroyed, killed by the sons of Jacob. For once they had fallen so drastically, their children would not have been salvable (AC 4493:5,6). The Lord always provides for our salvation or our freedom to be saved.

This remnant of the Most Ancient Church turned to the sensuous plane and sensuous evil. Here they were met and slain by an entirely sensuous people. With the Israelitish/Jewish Church, and indeed with the Christian and New Churches, there is from heredity a strong tendency toward evil in our sensuous level. In fact, tendencies to evil are present in the hereditary will on every plane, but especially in the sensuous. The Lord came on earth to confront this fallen condition and to show us the path to freedom and a return to true ideals.

In Genesis 3:15, the Lord God said: "And I will put enmity between you [the serpent] and the woman, and between your seed and her seed; He shall bruise your head, and you shall bruise His heel."

"He" is the Lord, come on earth. It is His heel, His sensuous, that is bruised by the serpent. But He conquers that serpent, and rises glorified on Easter.

The supreme sense of this story teaches of the Lord's clear sight of the sensuous evils active in His finite heredity through Mary. What might this sad story be describing about Jesus' inner process? Jesus has just now completed the process of making His natural-level consciousness Divine. The final level to face is the sensuous level, the most corrupted level of humankind.

And yet, ideally, the level of the senses should provide a beautiful link to the deepest, holiest parts of the soul. We see this pictured in infancy when a baby experiences all love and discovery directly through the senses.

When Jesus focuses His consciousness onto the level of human sensuality, He knows from within Him the beautiful links that are possible to join the senses with Divinity. Might He, in His finite and not yet glorified state of mind, be tempted to force the union between Divinity and human sensual experience, just as Shechem forced Dinah? We are shown in Luke 4:3 that Jesus was vulnerable to this kind of temptation, when the devil tempted Him in the wilderness to "Command this stone to become bread"; in other words, to "force people to be what you want them to be." And yet, though Jesus can be tempted in this way because of His great desire for our happiness, He does not give in. His Divine Soul knows well that to force anything upon human beings would be to remove their freedom and thus their very humanity. His human essence (the spiritual-celestial within Him) knows compulsion cannot lead to a true union. It is an appearance flowing in through His maternal human that tempts Him here.

Sadly, there is a shocking realization in store for Jesus in the human sensuous level, which He experiences through the finite maternal heredity He has received. In the human sensuous level, there is violent opposition and hatred toward any deeper kind of love and truth. Here there exists a hellish desire to reject, corrupt, and destroy celestial and spiritual matters, just as the sons of Jacob wickedly tricked, plundered, and destroyed this nation of the Hivites.

Seeing this causes Him deepest sadness, as when on earth He weeps when He regards Jerusalem and its fallen state. **This sadness is reflected in Genesis by Jacob's grief after his sons had committed this horrible slaughter: "Ye have troubled me, to make me to stink to the inhabitants of the land. . ." (Gen. 34:30).** His heredity through Mary embodies the hereditary fall of humankind. Seeing the evils within the sensuous, Jesus determines to face the glorification of this level within Himself out of love for us.

Chapter Twenty-Four

FULL GLORIFICATION OF THE NATURAL

BETHEL, BENJAMIN, AND ESAU'S GENEALOGY
GENESIS 35 AND 36

+ God appears to Jacob and tells him to go to Bethel. Jacob does so, and builds there an altar to God.

+ God blesses Jacob and again names him Israel.

+ Jacob and his family leave Bethel for Ephrath.

+ During the journey Rachel has hard labor, giving birth to Benjamin before she dies.

+ They arrive at Hebron where Jacob's father Isaac, lives. Isaac is very old, and he dies.

+ Esau's genealogy is given in Genesis 36.

Bethel was a sacred place to Jacob: here he had the dream of the ladder with angels ascending and descending and the Lord standing above it. Now, decades later, "God said unto Jacob, 'Arise, go up to Bethel, and abide there; and make there an altar unto God who appeared unto you when you fled from before Esau your brother'" (Gen. 35:1). Reflected here is the circle of life in which one starts from a spiritual base, travels through a thousand states and changes, and in the end returns to that starting place, now as an entirely different person.

Jacob asked his household and all that were with him to "put away the gods of the stranger which are in the midst of you, and purify yourselves" (Gen. 35:2). This they did, and then journeyed onward.

". . .and a terror of God was upon the cities that were round about them, and they did not pursue the sons of Jacob. And Jacob came to Luz, which is in the land of Canaan, this is Bethel. . . .And he built there an altar. . . .And God was seen by Jacob again when he came from Paddan-aram, and God blessed him. And God said unto him, 'Your name is Jacob; your name shall no more be called Jacob, but Israel shall be your name'; and He called his name Israel" (Gen. 35:2-10 selections).

Once before, after wrestling with the angel, Jacob was named Israel. This second naming, now by God, is an affirmation, and spiritually it is confirmation of a new state. With Jesus, this is an entry into the Divine Love itself in the natural plane of life.

Jacob's family journeyed from Bethel towards Ephrath, which is Bethlehem. Rachel then began labor with her final child, and she "suffered hard things in her bringing forth" (Gen. 35:16). "The midwife said unto her, 'Fear not, for this is also to you a son.' And it came to pass as her soul was going forth that she was about to die; and she called his name 'Benoni'; and his father called him 'Benjamin.' And Rachel died, and was buried in the way to Ephrath; this is Bethlehem" (Gen. 35:16-18, selections).

In the story Rachel's death is a tragedy. She was the most important person in Jacob's life, the one he loved deeply. However, Benjamin's birth is representatively a warm and beautiful thing. In the spiritual sense, Rachel's death and Benjamin's birth represent new and beautiful states. The birth of Benjamin signifies a breakthrough in the Lord's glorification in which He gains insights of truth which enable Him to enter a new and higher state. So with us: if only Benjamin can be born in our hearts, we find interior life and heavenly creativity. Benjamin is the medium, the step upward, to a higher heaven!

Benjamin was born near Ephrath, the earliest name for Bethlehem itself. That he was born here is no accident. Here also King David and the Lord Himself were born. For Bethlehem, like Benjamin, represents a miraculous stage of rebirth. For us it is the place where the Lord comes to us, where He is born as an infant in our hearts.

The qualities represented by Bethlehem and Benjamin have to do with the inner heavens, with angels who are sensitive and gentle and innocent. The Lord Himself achieves these qualities in a Divine way. The residue in His natural that has not been glorified is now becoming Divine. Benjamin's birth represents a progression with Jesus that is more interior and reaches up into His rational level where a new glory is born (AC 4536; 4585:2).

In the Lord's glorification, "Jacob" becomes "Israel." The Divine truth that He took to Himself (Jacob) becomes, after many states, the Divine Good (Israel). To Him, in His glorification, Rachel dies, and Benjamin is born. We can comprehend what these things mean only in a limited way. In us, Jacob's becoming Israel, and Rachel's death and Benjamin's birth near Bethlehem, speak of a gradual entering into gentleness and innocence and new warmth of love. These states come to us only from the angels and finally only from the Lord, and they promise closeness in our marriage and nearness to the Lord that we do not yet know. The residue on our natural level is reborn, and a miraculous new insight of truth (Benjamin) is born.

Bethlehem and Benjamin symbolize a step beyond the regeneration of the natural level. Benjamin brings sparkling truth to us. This truth is "new" in the sense that we see it with a clarity and insight we have never experienced before. It is seen in this new way because this truth comes from a higher, inmost good. Here then is a breakthrough — it leads to being an angel of the middle heaven, close to the Lord.

The states represented by Joseph and Benjamin come through the process of rebirth, and they come by the Lord's gift to us of victory in temptations. Rachel's giving birth to Benjamin, and suffering hard things in this birth, represent such temptations (AC 4586). The Lord is within this hard state, protecting and moderating.

Israel journeys now towards Hebron, where Isaac, his father, dwells. Prior to meeting Isaac, Israel's twelve sons are named again. But they are listed in an order different from that of their births, signifying a different subordination and ordering in the human mind, and, more importantly, in Jesus' mind. The *natural level has now been glorified* and is preparing for unification and integration with the Divine rational level, with Isaac. In the progress of glorification and rebirth, Jacob's ladder is continually activated: with Jesus Christ and in human rebirth, there is ascending and descending.

"Jacob came unto Isaac his father in Mamre Kiriatharba; this is Hebron, where Abraham and Isaac sojourned. And the days of Isaac were a hundred years and eighty years. And Isaac expired and died, and was gathered unto his people, old and sated of days; and Esau and Jacob his sons buried him" (Gen. 35:27).

The natural level of the Lord's mind is a receptacle for His rational. Now both are Divine, and with this comes a profound integration, a coming into One. Both are One, Jehovah, the Lord Jesus Christ. In this integration, Isaac — the rational as a separate entity — dies, old and sated of days. His two sons bury his body lovingly.

Spiritually, as with Rachel, this death is not a tragedy. Rather, it represents *new* life (AC 4618). Here then is an integration of tremendous impact. With Jesus Christ now comes an ascent from the glorified natural to the glorified rational, and an integration. Then He comes to these levels in us anew, with a power never before present (AC 4603). For this the angels sang. Yet there is still a level of glorification to be accomplished, that of His sensuous level, and His body.

The *Arcana* treatment of Genesis 36 is one of the shortest chapters in the whole work. This brevity is not due to lack of Divine content. Rather, it is because the subject, the glorification, is almost too profound for human comprehension. Literally the subject is **a full genealogy of the descendants of Esau who moved to the country of Edom.**

Esau in Edom represents the Divine good inflowing from the infinite Jehovah to be conjoined with the good in the natural represented by Jacob/Israel. It is a coming together of Divinity and glorified Humanity in Jesus Christ on earth, in His natural. Think of the incredible power of Infinite good coming down to become One with glorified good in Jesus Christ!

Esau stands now for that unique inner plane of Divine good in Jesus Christ that came from God. Jacob/Israel is the Divine good that by glorification replaces the hereditary evil in the Lord's finite human through Mary. These two become One (AC 4641). Divinity meets Humanity. This completes the glorification of the natural. It paves the way for a whole new subject: Joseph and his life from seventeen years old and onward.

The whole order of the Lord's Divinely good natural level is described by the descendants of Esau listed in Genesis 36. Even though our finite minds understand little within this genealogy, it is useful to read it, for if we read in a state of worship, an inflowing sphere of love from the Lord benefits both the angels and us.

It is the same with the genealogies of the Lord Jesus Christ in the New Testament: when people on earth read these in a state of worship and humility, angels are deeply moved. Something of the highest internal senses affects them with a flame of love. We may perceive the spiritual meanings only "as faint outlines" (AC 4644), but these can affect us. We can know from the treatment of Genesis 36 in the *Arcana* that now Divinity and Humanity in the Lord's natural are one. Because of this, our own limited natural levels can be reborn.

Chapter Twenty-Five

OVERVIEW OF THE GLORIFICATION OF THE SENSUOUS

JOSEPH: HIS DREAMS AND BETRAYAL
GENESIS 37

- ✦ Jacob gives a coat of many colors to his son Joseph.
- ✦ Joseph dreams symbolic dreams that his family will bow down to him.
- ✦ Later, Joseph's brothers betray him and sell him into slavery. They cause their father to believe that Joseph is dead.

Joseph's life story contains both an innocence and a promise that no other patriarch's story conveys. Joseph's dreams, his betrayal by his brothers, his exile to Egypt, and his miraculous rise to authority there, have a quality of wonder. One senses a symbolism in his life story. The book of Daniel also has this same enchanted sphere. Daniel's rise to power, his interpretations of dreams, and his miraculous escape from death also seem to suggest hidden messages. Spiritually, Joseph represents the Lord and our coming into love of Him.

Joseph's life completes the series of the four patriarchs. It also brings to an end the book of Genesis. Abraham's life, spiritually viewed, depicts the Lord's childhood. Isaac's life depicts the coming of the Divine rational to the Lord. Jacob, later renamed Israel, is the Divine natural. Joseph completes the series. His life depicts the coming of glorification to the sensuous level, and even the body, of the Lord Jesus Christ on earth (AC 4675, 5078, 4670).

After Joseph's brothers betrayed him and sold him into Egypt, they took his coat and dipped it in the blood of a goat they had killed. They brought this blood-stained coat of many colors to Jacob their father, and said: " 'This we have found; know now whether it be your son's tunic or not?' And Jacob knew it, and said, 'It is my son's tunic; an evil wild beast has devoured him; Joseph is torn in pieces' " (Gen. 37:32,33). Jacob was devastated; his beloved son was dead. Joseph's brothers also began in time to believe that Joseph was dead. Ten of them knew they had sold him away, and after many years they came to feel that he had died as a slave in Egypt.

We feel a haunting quality in his family's belief that Joseph was dead. For Joseph represents not only love of the Lord but also the innocence from infancy in each of us. In earliest childhood, we learn to love the Lord completely. We trust Him with our whole hearts and feel a tender and magical love for Him. But as we grow up and become adults, this earliest innocence and trust are forgotten. Tender remains are withdrawn into our interiors, above our conscious mind. As we discover evils in the world and in ourselves, we lose our earlier dreams and hopes. We feel Joseph is dead. We can come into our own rational faith (Isaac) and we can even find love of the neighbor in our natural lives (Jacob becoming Israel). But we simply know that Joseph is dead. Our inmost dreams of innocence and trust in the Lord fade. But the secret of the Joseph story is that *he does not die*. He can be restored to the central position in our hearts, even as this occurred with the Lord Jesus Christ at the end of His glorification.

If Joseph's life story portrays the rebirth of the sensuous level in us, isn't that the very lowest step in regeneration or rebirth? How is it that what is most ultimate or exterior marks the completion of the process of becoming an angel? The reason is that there is a surprising linkage between the senses and the celestial, or inmost, level in the human mind. We see this linking of the celestial and the sensuous with little infants. Tiny children live in a world of the senses, yet the highest angels surround them. The senses and the celestial are linked. Rebirth takes place on dual levels: as we ascend nearer to the Lord through regeneration, the Lord also brings order and rebirth to lower and lower levels of our minds (AC 5122:2; 5202:4; 5145; CL 302). In human rebirth, as in the Lord's glorification, we see a simultaneous ascent and descent, like the angels on Jacob's ladder.

Conjugial love is also an example of the linking of the celestial and the sensuous. If there is true order in a marriage, there is an ascent to ever-higher levels of the mind, with an effort even to a union of the souls (see CL 302). At the same time, there is a descent toward the senses. That is, tender states of love are expressed with affectionate touch and union in marriage. While conjugial love in its inmosts is a celestial love (CL 64), it is also a love that expresses itself gently through the senses.

In Joseph's first dream, the eleven sheaves that bowed down to him are his eleven brothers. In his second dream (as his father Jacob clearly saw) the sun and moon and eleven stars are Joseph's father, mother, and eleven brothers bowing before him. These dreams reveal that Joseph (that is, the quality represented by Joseph) is supreme, and that all other qualities bow down before this. With the Lord Himself, in His glorification, all other qualities in His mind bowed down before Joseph. Joseph now becomes the central figure — the love of Jehovah operative within Jesus. Joseph represents the wonderful, caring love within Jesus in this state, when the glorification of His sensuous and body are about to take place. In Swedenborg's Writings this love is called the "celestial of the spiritual," and it involves both the love of His Father or Divine Soul and His love for the salvation of humankind; this is also called His "human essence."

The evil heredity through Mary is still present and powerful in the sensuous level of Jesus' life on earth. It is active now, in this series, opposing further glorification. This heredity is the serpent that bruised Jesus' heel (Gen. 3:15), the "heel" being His sensuous.

Joseph's dreams prophesy the future state when spiritually the eleven sheaves of the field would bow before him as would the sun, moon, and stars. This foretells the glorification state when all qualities in the Lord's Human would become subordinate to the Divine love. This would happen when Divine love was fully received, and it would order all things in Jesus Christ. Then all the knowledges of good and truth within the Lord bow down before Divine love.

But at first this is *not* happening. Joseph's brothers, key qualities in the lower level of the Lord's mind, do *not* bow down. They resist, reject, and hate the celestial, even as nine of Joseph's brothers were jealous of him and despised him. (Benjamin and Reuben did not share in this hatred.)

This speaks clearly of a strong need in the process of the Lord's glorification, the need for the evils in His maternal heredity that reject the Divine love to be removed, extirpated. Until this is done, the glorification is incomplete. Now Joseph, instead of ruling, is sent into slavery and exile. Joseph himself must experience trials and temptations, for the celestial of the spiritual, although it is a wondrous quality, is not yet Divine or glorified in Jesus (see AC 5256, 5257).

The nine sons of Jacob who despised Joseph now represent those qualities that are dominated spiritually by sensuous pleasure apart from any higher loves (AC 4769:1). Perhaps here the nine brothers of Joseph represent in the supreme sense the hereditary evils and falsities in the sensuous level of the Lord: these are tendencies to evils and falsities that exist through His finite maternal heredity.

Here we come to the last major stage of the Lord's glorification, with the goal of its completion. Does the "Joseph" stage of Jesus' development happen at the same time as His public ministry? Might the physical healing He gave during His travels, often by means of the sense of touch, have happened at the same time as His inner battles to bring healing to the human sensuous level? Perhaps future studies of this subject will shed more light on this possibility.

Now is when the Lord's worst temptations take place. The evils of humankind that have access to Jesus through His maternal heredity flow most powerfully through the sensuous heredity. Certainly in the temptations in the garden of Gethsemane and on the cross, the serpent bruises Jesus' heel.

Chapter Twenty-Six

THE BETRAYAL BY THE HEREDITARY SENSUOUS

JOSEPH'S BROTHERS BETRAY HIM
GENESIS 37 CONTINUED

+ Joseph is sent to help his brothers with the flock of sheep.

+ When his brothers see him coming, they decide to kill him because they are jealous of his dreams.

+ Instead of killing him they sell him to some passing Midianite traders as a slave.

+ The brothers take Joseph's tunic, dipped in goat's blood, back to their father Jacob. Jacob believes that Joseph is dead, and he mourns.

+ The Midianites sell Joseph in Egypt to Potiphar, an official of Pharaoh.

Joseph was seventeen when he had the two dreams foretelling his future role. When he was sent to his brothers, who were tending the sheep at Dothan, his brothers did not warmly greet him, but laid a plan to kill him instead. Reuben intervened and discouraged this plan. Yet still, when Joseph came to them, the nine brothers grabbed him roughly, stripped him of

his coat of many colors, and threw him into a barren pit. Later, Judah noticed Ishmaelites passing by in a caravan and suggested that Joseph be sold to them for profit.

Joseph's brothers sold him into Egypt for twenty pieces of silver. Celestial angels, when they hear stories from the Word, search out the inmost affections involved, for these are the keys to the internal meaning. This story causes horror to the angels. To them Joseph is the Lord, Who came innocently to humankind. The evil within humankind first intends to kill the Lord, but then instead, out of greed, representatively sells Him. **Joseph's tunic was misused to prove his death to Jacob.** Here is raw hatred, intended murder, and greed, together with the lie about the tunic, and the terrible devastation of Jacob because of this lie.

Towards Jesus Himself, in His goal of the glorification of the sensuous, the hells show violent opposition, especially the lowest hell, the genii. As we have seen, Jesus, working through the "celestial of the spiritual" (Joseph), looks to glorifying His sensuous level and His body. The "celestial of the spiritual" is a deep love of Jehovah, along with a deep love of humankind. He knows what this process will do for humankind, for each of us. He knows it will open up the choice of heaven for us in a way never before possible, enabling us to see and love the Lord even with our sensuous mind.

But the hells resist violently. They infiltrate the Lord's states through His maternal human heredity. In this lower human are all the evils of humankind in potentiality. The hells rise to attack. They take Jesus, coming in innocence, throw Him into a barren pit, and finally sell Him into Egypt. His coat they abuse to prove His death.

Looking at Joseph's story, and at Jesus' later life on earth as recounted in the New Testament, we see similarities. Jesus also is betrayed, but in His case it is the Pharisees and Judas who betray Him. Judas sells Him for thirty pieces of silver, as Judah sold Joseph for twenty pieces of silver. The Lord's outer coat is taken, gambled for by lots, and won by a Roman soldier. His enemies put

Jesus to death, and Joseph's brothers nearly put him to death. Joseph in the pit, without water, is like Jesus in his final temptations, when He is in a spiritual pit and says, "I thirst" (John 19:28). What happened to Joseph here is then a prophecy of future temptations in the Lord's own life.

In brief, the maternal heredity in the Lord rejected the celestial of the spiritual (Joseph). Love of the Lord wears a beautiful coat of many colors. These colors are the wonderful varieties of natural sciences and arts that clothe the reality of the one Lord (AC 4667). But evil takes this clothing of affirming facts, dips it in the blood of misinterpretation, and conveys it with arrogance: "Look, here are your so-called facts that clothe the Lord's reality." Evil cunningly misuses nature, science, and the arts to disprove the Lord's existence. And evil then sells the Lord into Egypt as just another knowledge, in this case as evil and empty knowledge.

Because of a different emphasis in the two series, the amounts for which Joseph in the Old Testament and the Lord in the New Testament are betrayed are not the same. The twenty pieces of silver for which Joseph was sold represent low estimation of Joseph's spiritual value, a rejection of remains or innocence, and a turning to what is unholy (AC 4759). The thirty pieces of silver for which the Lord was betrayed by Judas represent those who "value so little the Lord's merit, and redemption and salvation by Him" (AC 2276). The two amounts are spiritually related and fill out each other's meaning. In either case, the highest love is sold for greed.

It seems that the Divine natural (Jacob), in temptation, is attacked by the appearance that humankind will never tame its sensuous. It appears here that the hells win and the highest human love (Joseph) perishes before these lowest evils. Seeing the bloodstained tunic, Jacob believes Joseph to be dead.

Chapter Twenty-Seven

LOVE OF DOMINION IN THE HEREDITARY SENSUOUS

JUDAH AND TAMAR
GENESIS 38

+ Jacob's son Judah marries a Canaanite woman and has three sons: Er, Onan, and Shelah.

+ Judah arranges for Er, his oldest, to marry Tamar, but Er dies before producing any children.

+ According to Israelitish law, Onan must marry his brother's widow and raise up children for him.

+ Onan marries Tamar, but he also dies with no offspring. Tamar is told to wait for Shelah to grow up for her next husband.

+ Judah's wife dies. Tamar, who desires her right for children, disguises herself and waits by the road for Judah. Judah thinks she is a harlot, and goes in to her.

+ Judah learns that Tamar has become pregnant. He orders that she be killed for harlotry, not knowing that he is the father.

+ When Judah learns the truth, he spares Tamar and she delivers twins: Perez and Zerah.

Genesis now tells the strange story of Judah and his daughter-in-law Tamar. In this story Judah takes on an evil representation: the lowest evil in the Lord's maternal heredity, the love of dominion. The Lord sees the quality of this love in all its terrible forms. It is the extreme of the evil love of self. Delight in ruling and dominating over others on the sensual level is the most powerful natural delight the hells offer. Its appeal has undermined many human souls. It comes in subtle disguises. It puts concern for self above all else: above one's spouse, family, country, and church. The Lord's first concern is for what this evil may do to humankind, how it might spiritually destroy the human race on this earth. His fear from His love (see AC 2034) is that His mission on earth will fail because humankind will be overcome by the evil represented by Judah. How valid this concern is may be confirmed by studying the contemporary world where all kinds of minor wars, power struggles, and brutal crimes dominate our newscasts.

The Judah quality that attacks the Lord comes to Him through the sensuous degree. This is where Judah particularly nestles. The desire to dominate and the sensuous are joined together. So with us also. This evil is manifested in rape, incest, and the sexual abuse of children. Jesus felt horror at seeing this potential quality in His maternal heredity and therefore in humankind. This with most of us is likely only a tendency, deeply hidden in the unconscious. But to know its potential is to lessen its possibility of openly attacking us.

"Judah saw. . .a daughter of a man, a Canaanite, and her name was Shua; and he took her, and came to her" (Gen. 38:2). In time, and in following order, three sons were born of this marriage: Er, Onan, and Shelah. "Judah took a woman for Er his firstborn, and her name was Tamar" (Gen. 38:6). There is about Tamar, probably from her good correspondence here, a sense of beauty and loveliness. Tamar represents a church that is genuine, one whose spirit has innocence and humility (AC 4831). "The internal of the church here is Tamar, and its external is Judah with his three sons by the Canaanite woman" (*Ibid.*). Judah and his sons are not only the external elements of the church but also an external that has no soul, no true internal.

Tamar was first given to Er as a "woman" or wife, but he was evil, and died without offspring. It was an Israelitish custom that a brother was obligated to provide offspring if his brother died with none. **Tamar was then given to Onan who died after refusing to beget offspring for his brother. Judah did not want his third son, Shelah, to die also. He asked Tamar to return to her father's house and wait until Shelah grew up, but he really had no intention of fulfilling this obligation. When Shelah was grown, Judah withheld him from marriage to Tamar. When it became clear that Judah would never keep his promise to give Shelah in marriage to her, Tamar disguised herself as a harlot, and after Judah's wife died, enticed him to ask her, as a harlot, for intercourse. He did not know her identity. When Tamar became pregnant from this union, Judah would have killed her for unfaithfulness until he learned that he himself was the father.**

The love of dominion is hell's lowest and strongest love. This rejects what is genuine even as Judah rejected Tamar as a wife for Shelah and took her for himself as a harlot. That he did this unknowingly tells even more about his state representatively: love of ruling does not care that it treats genuine loves (Tamar) as a harlot (AC 4868:2). Such, too, is the coldness in sensuous dominion that allows rape and incest, or sexual domination in marriage.

Perhaps in the supreme sense Judah is the tendency to sensuous evil in the Lord's maternal heredity (AC 4825, 4868:2). This hereditary evil could not be conjoined with anything genuine. To the Lord this is a great sadness. He sees the evil in humankind inrooted in its sensuous level, as it is in His maternal heredity. If only this plane were pure, as it had been in Most Ancient times! Then Tamar, all that is lovely, could have been conjoined with Judah's son in a conjugial marriage. Instead, the sensual level of humanity refused to join with something genuine and internal, as Judah and his sons refused to provide Tamar with a husband and offspring.

The birth of the twins to Tamar represents the beginning of the glorification of the Lord's sensuous level, which is done by introducing genuine qualities of truth and goodness to this level. This representation takes Judah's union with Tamar in its best light. The sensuous level (Judah), which refused to join legitimately with something deeper (Tamar), is coaxed into a first union that does indeed produce some results. The twin boys born to Tamar, Zerah and Perez, symbolize states of goodness and truth that begin the Lord's process of bringing rebirth to the sensuous level.

Jesus knows that the real power to bring the sensuous level back in line with heaven lies in the power of goodness. This acknowledgment of the power of goodness is symbolized by the fact that **the infant Zerah (goodness in the sensuous) first thrust his hand out of his mother's womb, and a midwife tied around it a cord of double-dyed scarlet.**

And yet Zerah pulls his hand back into the womb, and his brother Perez is born first. Perez symbolizes truth in the sensuous level. Jesus sees that the human sensuous level is so devoid of goodness that He must first use truth to set it back into order. In the process of regeneration we too must first use the power of truth to teach our sensual level how to live in goodness.

The message of Genesis 38 is that Jesus Christ puts Divine truth firmly into practice on the sensuous level where His maternal human heredity wishes to rule. Jesus finds the means that will gradually lead to goodness on the sensuous plane. He does this by calling upon His own Divine remains of goodness, from His earliest states of innocence when He was an infant, living completely and innocently in the sensuous plane.

Chapter Twenty-Eight

EARLY TEMPTATIONS IN THE SENSUOUS

JOSEPH AND POTIPHAR'S WIFE
GENESIS 39

+ Joseph proves to be a skilled and loyal servant for Potiphar. Potiphar puts Joseph in charge of his household and possessions.

+ Potiphar's wife yearns for Joseph, and tries to entice him into an adulterous relationship.

+ Joseph refuses, and this makes Potiphar's wife furious. She openly accuses Joseph of trying to rape her.

+ Potiphar is enraged, and throws Joseph into prison.

+ But even in prison, Jehovah gives Joseph "favor in the sight of the keeper of the prison." The keeper places Joseph in charge of all the other prisoners.

When Joseph was sold into Egypt, Potiphar, captain of Pharaoh's guard, purchased him as a servant. Here "Jehovah was with Joseph" (Gen. 39:2). In time he was set over Potiphar's house and all that he had. But once again he was

**betrayed, this time by Potiphar's wife, and then unjustly put
into prison. Here also "Jehovah was with Joseph" (Gen. 39:21).
Soon he supervised all things in the prison, having won the
complete trust of its head keeper.**

Joseph represents the Lord's highest human essence on earth
before this is glorified and made Divine. This human essence has
two combining qualities: truth and good on a very high level, or the
spiritual and the celestial. In doctrinal terminology, Joseph is the
"celestial of the spiritual" (AC 4962), a love both for Jehovah and
for saving humankind.

Thus Joseph is that "pure love" (AC 1812) towards the human
race which motivates the Lord on earth. Joseph and his younger
brother Benjamin are closely linked together in the Word because
spiritually they combine as a one (AC 4592:2). These two as one
are the human essence of the Lord before He is completely glorified — with Benjamin representing new truth seen as sparkling and
alive, which flows from the celestial love, which is Joseph.

**Jehovah was with Joseph, and all that Joseph did pros-
pered.** So too does that celestial of the spiritual within Jesus. As the
glorification progresses, this pure love prospers and advances,
going through initial states preparatory to the glorification of the
Lord's sensuous level. Jesus (Joseph) is spiritually in the land of
Egypt (natural level knowledges) in order to face sensuous elements in His nature and to glorify these.

But this does not happen without severe temptations. The
Word says, **"Joseph was beautiful in form and beautiful in
appearance" (Gen. 39:6).** So is the celestial of the spiritual, that
high love within the Lord: it is beauty itself. It is then with a sense
of shock that we read: **"And it happened. . .after these events,
that his lord's [Potiphar's] wife lifted up her eyes towards
Joseph, and said, 'Lie with me' " (Gen. 39:7). Joseph refused,
saying, "How. . .shall I do this great evil and sin against God?"
(Gen. 39:9). But Potiphar's wife insistently demanded this day**

after day, until one day when Joseph came into the house, which was then deserted of others, "she took hold of him by the garment, saying, 'Lie with me.' And Joseph left his garment in her hand, and fled, and went out of doors" (Gen. 39:11,12).

Adultery is one of the worst of evils. Representatively with Potiphar's wife, this is not a natural or physical adultery that is being spoken about. It is an attack by the hells on the inner level of the sensuous with the Lord Himself. Perhaps when Joseph flees and leaves his garment in her hand, this is an early prophecy about the Lord Himself when He was being led away to be crucified.

"Then the soldiers, when they had crucified Jesus, took His garments and made four parts, to each soldier a part, and also the tunic. Now the tunic was without seam, woven from the top in one piece. They said therefore among themselves, 'Let us not tear it, but cast lots for it'. . . .Therefore the soldiers did these things" (John 19:23,24).

Potiphar's wife was furious at Joseph's rejection: the anger of a lusting woman scorned. She shouted in feigned horror and then displayed Joseph's garment and claimed that he had tried to rape her. She later told Potiphar this, and he in hot anger had Joseph "committed. . .to the prison house" (Gen. 39:20). Potiphar's wife represents the evil passion of the hells now attacking the Lord, here the evil spirits of the milder hells (AC 5035e). But the genii, the lowest devils, are behind these evil spirits. The attack was directly against Jesus, against His love for our salvation (AC 5042).

The method of this attack is the temptation to engage in adultery: here, in the internal representation, spiritual adultery, which is to have a true love undermined by a lower lust. This has its foundation in natural or physical adultery.

In the celestial sense this chapter is speaking of the Lord Jesus Christ in the later states of His life on earth. I believe this is when

He walked and taught and healed in the land of Canaan. The love that is to be glorified is the celestial of the spiritual which is His pure love for the salvation of human beings (AC 1812, 2034). This love is now under attack at the sensuous level.

The attempted adultery of Potiphar's wife depicts milder hells focusing Jesus' attention on the horrifying depravity of the sensuous level with humankind. Putting this in my own words, the hells ask: "How can this depraved sensuous level survive temptations of spiritual and natural adultery? Your sensuous as inherited through Mary is incapable of glorification; it is completely fallen and depraved." The Lord answered this by continuing His glorification of this very level by saying in effect, "Get behind Me, Satan" (Matt. 16:23).

Throughout this process, the Lord's human essence is being glorified. It is not the internal level alone (the celestial of the spiritual) that is now being glorified. It is this internal as it is present in the lowest of the natural: in the sensuous itself (AC 5086). This ongoing glorification of the Lord's sensuous is vital for us, for so often it is abuse of the senses that betrays us. If He glorifies His sensuous, He makes it possible for Him to regenerate our own sensuous level. This knowledge is vital in overcoming attacks that come through our senses: alcoholism, drug abuse, child abuse, and even adultery. We can and must, as the Alcoholics Anonymous organization teaches, turn "to a Higher Power."

Here then is the Lord's love coming down to the sensuous to bring glorification there. Isn't this where we especially need Him? Isn't it too often true of us that the "spirit indeed is willing, but the flesh is weak" (Matt. 26:41)?

One clear indication that the sensuous is the focus here is that the story happens in Egypt, which represents ultimate knowledges that come in through the senses (AC 5078:4). The Lord's goal here is to make the whole of His body Divine, including His organs of sensation (AC 5078:2). "He rose from the grave with His body, and after the resurrection told the disciples, 'See My hands and My feet, that it is I Myself; handle Me and see; for a spirit does not have flesh and bones as you see Me have' " (*Ibid.*).

Potiphar had Joseph cast into prison. There, once again, Jehovah came to his aid. He was given leadership responsibility over the whole prison. "And whatever he did, Jehovah made it to prosper" (Gen. 39:23).

That Joseph was with those who were imprisoned means representatively that the Lord is in temptations. Yet the celestial of the spiritual in Him rules and holds steady even in these terrible temptations. He fights alone from His own power, unlike any other person on earth (AC 5045). These trials are leading up to His final temptation on the cross and to the greatest victory, when His Human becomes Divine. Then the Joseph within Him, the celestial of the spiritual, will be glorified. All of the Divine Providence leads toward this.

Chapter Twenty-Nine

The Setting for Jesus' Sensuous Temptation

The Butler and the Baker
Genesis 40

+ Pharaoh's chief butler and baker offend their king, and thus are put into the same prison where Joseph is being held.

+ The prince of the guards places Joseph in charge of these other two prisoners.

We come next to the story of Joseph in prison with Pharaoh's butler and baker, and of their dreams (Genesis 40). The inner meaning of this historical account deals with the glorification of the senses: the process of Divinity coming to the lowest level of Jesus Christ.

In this story Pharaoh, king of Egypt, symbolizes the Lord's natural-level mind that has now been glorified. But there are tendencies in the Lord's sensuous mind, represented by the butler and the baker, that are in great disorder from His finite maternal heredity.

When God originally created human beings, He created our senses to serve and reflect our love of God and love of other people. Thus heaven itself could be felt right down in our bodies. But over time, human beings used the senses more and more to pursue selfish, empty, and harmful pleasures that shut out heaven altogether. Sensuous thinking and delights were no longer used to serve higher thinking and loves, but instead to shut out and dominate them. The Writings describe the ideal position of sensual experience in our lives:

"When sensory impressions occupy [a subordinated] position, happiness and bliss radiate from the interior man into the delights of the senses and make these delights *a thousand times better* than they were before" (AC 5125:2, italics added).

When God came on earth as Jesus, He made this possible again, if we choose to follow His path.

Since the corrupted elements in the human sensuous mind, represented by the butler and the baker, are so opposed to the purity of the Divine Natural level in Jesus (Pharaoh), they cannot remain near this level. This is represented in the literal story by the fact that **the butler and the baker had sinned against their king, and were thus cast into prison** (AC 5079, 5083). This prison symbolizes a state of falsity from evil (AC 5085).

It was not human sensations themselves that were rejected by the Divine Natural. Rather it was the views, thoughts, affections, and desires that people were drawing from the senses, which were opposed to the things of spiritual love and truth (AC 5094).

But there is a part of Jesus that is present right there in the midst of the corrupted human sensuous mind. This is Joseph, the celestial love that has come to rescue and restore this level, and lead it back toward heaven. **Joseph is there in prison with the butler and the baker.** Jesus' love is there, enduring the imprisonment of the temptations of sensuous evil in order that He may set us free.

Immediately, Pharaoh's prince of the guards places Joseph in charge of the other two prisoners. The prince of the guards represents true ideas from the deeper sense of the Word of God.

From these deep truths (the prince of the guards) Jesus uses His celestial love now present in this lower level (Joseph) to teach the human sensuous mind (AC 5087, 5088), working to guide it back toward serving goodness and truth.

Jesus confronts the hells on the level of the senses. He does this from the Joseph within Him, from the celestial of the spiritual. His human essence experiences spiritually the states that come to Joseph in the prison house. Jesus' love for the salvation of the human race is now focused on the human sensuous mind and how this should be Divinely ordered.

The senses are meant to be a tool for the inner or spiritual level to use while living in the natural world. But the external senses tend to take over and dominate the inner plane instead of the other way around. If this actually happens, and is confirmed, "a person is done for" (AC 5077). However, while we remain on earth, repentance is always possible. The Lord faces the hells on the plane of the senses as they inflow through His finite maternal heredity, and He shows the path in His ordering of these senses.

In the *Arcana* we read:

"The present chapter deals with how the Lord glorified or made Divine the exterior aspects of. . .[the] natural. The exterior aspects of the natural are rightly called bodily ones, being both kinds of sensory powers of perception together with their recipient members and organs; for these recipients together with those powers make up that which is referred to as the body. . .The Lord made Divine all that constituted His body, both its sensory powers and their recipient members and organs, which also explains why He rose from the grave with His body, and after the resurrection told His disciples, 'See My hands and My feet, that it is I Myself; handle Me, and see; for a spirit does not have flesh and bones as you see Me have' " (Luke 24:39; AC 5078:2).

The Lord alone glorified His body, or made it Divine (*Ibid.*). He made His body Divine for purposes we are just beginning to understand. It gives Him a retained power on the most ultimate plane. We are reassured that He has a Divine presence even on the plane of our bodies. Of course we can never regenerate our body; that is, the Lord does not look to this as His goal for us. For the natural body serves a temporary role here in this world while we make our free choices of good or evil, heaven or hell. After our physical bodies die, we are given spiritual bodies that are far more perfect and sensitive than the ones they replace.

However, Jesus glorified His senses and the complete sensuous level. "As Moses lifted up the serpent in the wilderness, even so must the Son of Man be lifted up, that whoever believes in Him should not perish but have eternal life" (John 3:14,15). The serpent is the sensuous, and this was "lifted up" or glorified with the Lord. "And I, if I am lifted up from the earth, will draw all peoples to Myself" (John 12:32).

Representatively, when the butler and baker sinned, it was against the true order within the natural level (here depicted by the king). This natural plane of the mind consists of "known facts and the affections for them" (AC 5079:2). Such things are being brought into order and glorified with Jesus (AC 5079). But the impressions flowing in through the senses are not yet ordered. They are open to the disarray of evil.

The challenge is to bring heavenly order to our senses. From infancy and early childhood we have affections and perceptions that are innocent and good. These heavenly remains are associated with our senses. So despite our evil heredity, which lodges in and works through the senses, we also have goods from infancy and childhood on this same level, making a potential equilibrium possible (see AC 1555).

The prison-house where the butler and baker and Joseph were all bound represents temptations regarding the senses and body. This is an apt representation, for prisons suggest a sphere of being bound, limited, and also a darkness of atmosphere. Sensuous temptations come to us throughout our adult lives. Inmost love (Joseph) is about to work with these senses, to instruct them, and to work with Providence to bring them into order. Illusions of the senses need to be deprived of power. "And the prince of the guards set Joseph over them" (Gen. 40:4). Under the guidance of principles from the Word (the prince of the guards), the celestial (Joseph) taught these sensories (see AC 5087). During these severe temptations it is inmost love, using the Word, that instructs and teaches our lowest level regarding the true uses of sensations.

In old age, the failing body brings difficulties and infirmities. These cause hard trials and temptations centered on the senses. This is true in serious illness as well. Other temptations may arise when health is good, and yet our minds and hearts are focused on outer sensations apart from love of others and the Lord. However, the greatest liberation also comes in old age. It is likened ideally in the Writings to a time of innocence and the wisdom of innocence, when from the Lord a person again becomes like a child, but now a wise child (see AC 10225). What is more touching than loving, innocent old people? The Lord is with them. In spirit they are like Simeon who held the baby Jesus in his arms.

Chapter Thirty

STEPS IN GLORIFYING THE SENSUOUS

THE DREAMS OF THE BUTLER AND THE BAKER
GENESIS 40 CONTINUED

- ✦ The butler and the baker each describes a dream to Joseph.
- ✦ Joseph interprets the dreams, gaining this knowledge from God. The interpretations describe the future fate of the butler and the baker.
- ✦ The fates that Joseph describes come to pass. The butler is restored to his former position, while the baker is executed.
- ✦ The butler forgets to ask Pharaoh to grant Joseph's freedom, as Joseph had asked him to.

The days that the butler and the baker spent in custody symbolize the long period in which the corrupted finite sensuous mind inherited by Jesus through Mary could not be in the presence of His glorified Divine Natural mind. Jesus' celestial love (Joseph) was working down in the prison of sensuous evil and temptations to teach and reform the human sensuous mind. But would these efforts be successful?

A revelation about the future comes to Jesus, represented by the dreams of the butler and the baker. **The dreams come to these two prisoners during the night, and in the morning they are sad because they do not know the meaning of the dreams.** In the part of His mind that is entangled in the impurities of finite human sensuous thinking (the butler and the baker, AC 5083, 5084, 5095) Jesus cannot foresee the outcome of His efforts. Can His work save this final level of humanity and restore it to accord with Divine order?

And then, in the morning, Joseph comes. The clarity of morning represents the ability of Jesus' celestial love (Joseph) to perceive the future fate of these two elements in the human sensuous mind. As Jesus perceives this knowledge through a revelation from His Divine Soul, so **Joseph perceives the meanings of the dreams through a revelation from God.**

The butler and the baker each represent different parts of the human sensuous mind (see AC 5157). The "butler" pictures knowledge that has been gained through the senses – thoughts, concepts, ideas. This part of the sensuous mind has connection with intellectual thought, and therefore it can be taught. For instance, one's eyes take in the sight of the sun rising and setting, and the sensuous mind can conclude that the sun moves around the earth. However, this sensuous thought can be altered or re-taught by the intellectual concept that the earth is rotating and orbiting, creating the illusion of a moving sun. Then the sensuous mind can understand why the eyes are seeing what they see. This part of the mind can grasp, "What you are seeing is not what it first appears to be." This type of sensuous thinking, governed by human understanding and represented by the butler, enters especially through the senses of sight and hearing, but also to some extent through smell and taste (AC 5077).

The baker, on the other hand, represents the part of the sensuous mind that experiences *delights* through the senses. This part of the mind functions apart from the intellect. If a person has established a feeling of delight in something disorderly, such as drinking

177

alcohol excessively, that part of his or her mind cannot be told, "You do not find pleasure in drinking excessively." The "baker" in our minds cannot comprehend anything beyond what it feels. A person must abandon and reject the behavior that feeds that harmful pleasure and replace it with new and higher sources of pleasure. Any recovering alcoholic knows that a return to previous harmful behaviors will bring that same destructive pleasure right back. This kind of purely sensuous perception, governed by the human hereditary will and represented by the baker, can enter through hearing, smell, or taste, but most especially through touch (AC 5077).

In a revelation from His Divine Soul, Jesus foresees what will become of these two parts of the fallen human sensuous mind. This revelation is described representatively by the dreams of the butler and the baker.

Special dreams in the Word involve Divine foresight, and this is the case with the dreams of the butler and baker (AC 5091). The Lord alone can foretell the future; not even angels have this faculty. Jehovah gave Jesus Christ on earth the ability of foresight; Jesus knew the future destiny of the senses within Himself. Joseph, who represents the human essence of the Lord, could foretell the meaning of the butler's and baker's dreams. **When Joseph said, "Do not interpretations belong to God?" (Gen. 40:8), he was saying that God gave him the ability to interpret.**

The butler told his dream to Joseph, and said to him:

" 'In my dream. . .behold, a vine before me. And on the vine three shoots, and it was as though budding; its blossoms came up, and its clusters ripened into grapes. And Pharaoh's cup was in my hand, and I took the grapes and pressed them into Pharaoh's cup, and put the cup onto Pharaoh's palm.' And Joseph said to him, 'This is the interpretation of it: The three shoots are three days. In yet three days Pharaoh will lift up your head and will restore you to your position, and you will put Pharaoh's cup into his hand, according to the former man-

ner when you were his cupbearer' " (Gen. 40:9-13).

In its inner meaning the butler's dream tells of the re-ordering of sensuous thinking that is subject to the understanding or intellect. Jesus foresees that this part of human sensuous thinking can be brought back into accord with higher thinking, at least for a time. The details of the dream describe how this comes about.

The **"shoots"** are derivatives from the understanding that extend down even to the senses, especially in the rebirth of the sense of sight (see AC 5114:1). The rebirth begins first with leaves that represent heavenly intelligence applied to these senses (subject to the understanding) which properly orders them. Then come **blossoms**, which are qualities not just of intelligence but of wisdom coming to the use of the senses.

Clusters are the truths coming to these senses when they look outward toward *good* to the neighbor. This happens when we use our senses not simply to provide enjoyment for ourselves, but to serve others with love. Finally come the **ripe grapes** or fruit, which are goods done from celestial truths (see AC 5117), that is, using the senses to promote love to the Lord, conjugial love, and love of little children (AC 2039)(AC 5116:5).

The butler was restored to serving Pharaoh after three days, but sadly he forgot Joseph and what Joseph had done for him. The senses subject to understanding were restored to order and received heavenly influx. But the glorification of the senses with the Lord and the rebirth of the senses of human beings (those subject to the understanding) are not completed; the butler forgot Joseph. A major step had been taken, but there are still further stages to come. The celestial still feels bound, forgotten in an inward prison.

"And when the chief of the bakers saw that Joseph had interpreted what was good, and he said to Joseph, 'I also was in my dream, and behold, three baskets with holes in them were on my head. And in the highest basket there were some of every

kind of food for Pharaoh, the work of the baker, and the birds were eating them out of the basket, from upon my head.' And Joseph answered and said, 'This is the interpretation of it: The three baskets are three days. In yet three days Pharaoh will lift up your head from upon you, and will hang you on wood; and the birds will eat your flesh from upon you'" (Gen. 40:16-19).

The subject now is the sensory degree subject to the will, represented by the baker (AC 5144). This is primarily the sense of touch, but also the senses of smell and taste, and to a degree, the sense of hearing (AC 5077:3). These senses have strong connections with the fallen hereditary will.

The three baskets that had "holes in them" depict the hereditary will. In this will are no receptive levels of conscience, nothing that would receive and retain the inflowing of good (or food) from the highest level. Our hereditary will loathes the idea of conscience on any level and it ridicules such things. There are holes in the baskets allowing food (goodness) to fall through and be corrupted in the lower levels. In this hereditary will, remains of childhood are not retained by either the civil or the spiritual level of conscience (AC 5145:3).

The primary area of operation of this fallen will is on the sensuous plane where it loves to work through touch, or smell and taste, and would also like to capture hearing and sight. It would lower these to lusts. It would dominate our senses. If this is achieved, then **the birds come and eat the food from the uppermost basket**: that is, lies or excuses originating in our evils pluck out and eat any inner goods.

The senses, obsessed by the fallen will, take a ruling position when food and drink take precedence over any higher values — when drugs mean more than revealed truth, when the body means more than the spirit. Many, many human beings have been caught in this bodily trap. We are all vulnerable. It is a primary way in which the hells can take us over. The bodily senses seem external and relatively unimportant, yet they are entry points for evil spirits who delight in destroying us.

The Divine will of Jesus is from His Soul. This will does not receive sensuous delights flowing in through the maternal heredity. Such delights are "evil, and therefore had to be cast aside" (AC 5157:3). **This is the baker who was hanged.** In His glorification, the Lord successively rejects and casts aside His finite maternal human. In place of the hereditary will through Mary, the Lord acquires a new will: this new will flows down to the level of His senses. In time, this very ultimate level will be glorified. His senses and even His body will be glorified (AC 5078:2).

Hereditary evil, allied with touch, would lead us to reject life after death. Touch could tell us that only our body is real. It would suggest strongly that when our body dies, we are wiped out forever. The hells, through the misuse of touch impressions, would lead us to utter despair. What the Lord is teaching here directly is that the "baker" is *lying*, distorting sense impressions. We can reject the lies he tells. The butler can be re-ordered in us, receiving new information about the heavenly use of the senses. We can understand the beauty of our earthly environment a "thousand times" more clearly than before. In place of the baker, a new will that is allied to all of our senses can be given us. The Lord glorified His senses; He can help us in the rebirth of ours.

For now, however, Joseph is still in prison. The butler has forgotten the interpreter of his dream, which means that the celestial is still imprisoned by false attitudes, false principles. **When Joseph says to the butler, "Remember me,"** he represents the celestial love of Jesus, urging His not-yet-glorified sensuous thinking to *remember* that the Divine exists in all physical and worldly issues. But this does not happen yet. **The butler does not speak to Pharaoh about Joseph in order to set him free.** The sensuous is not yet fully subordinate and in compliance with heavenly loves. Despite the elevation of the butler and the hanging of the baker, rebirths still must take place before the sensuous is in true order.

Toward the end of His life on earth, the Lord clearly foretold the coming crucifixion and His resurrection. The story of the baker is in one sense a prophecy of the final temptation on the cross when the maternal human would be cast aside, rejected. The elevation of the butler is a foretelling of the Divine resurrection to come.

The leading factor in the completion of the glorification, and of our regeneration, is innocence (AC 5168:2). This is prophesied with Jesus Christ on earth, when John the Baptist sees Him: "Behold the Lamb of God, Who takes away the sin of the world" (John 1:29).

Chapter Thirty-One

DIVINE CHANGES IN THE SENSUOUS

JOSEPH: TWICE REDEEMED
GENESIS 41

+ Pharaoh has two dreams that he does not understand.

+ The chief butler finally remembers Joseph in prison. He tells Pharaoh that this is a man who can interpret his dreams.

+ Joseph is brought up out of prison. From the power of God he interprets Pharaoh's dreams.

+ Pharaoh is so pleased that he sets Joseph in a great position of power, and gives him the daughter of the priest of On as wife.

Joseph was betrayed first by his brothers and then by Potiphar's wife, and as a final blow he was simply forgotten in prison by the butler. The betrayals and the forgetting portray the coldness of evil, which rejects the Savior of humankind. These rejections of Joseph, who represents the Lord, have their counterparts in the New Testament.

After Jesus is baptized by John, He is led up by the Spirit into the wilderness, and there endures three temptations. After He fasts forty days, the tempter asks Him to turn stones into bread: to force the stony hearts of people into being good. Then the devil takes Him up onto the pinnacle of the temple in Jerusalem, and says, "Throw yourself down. For it is written: 'He shall give His angels charge concerning you. . .In their hands they shall bear you up, lest you dash your foot against a stone" (Matt. 4:6). After Jesus conquers in this temptation, the devil takes Him up into an exceedingly high mountain, and offers Him all the kingdoms of the world if He will worship him. Jesus answers, "Away with you, Satan! For it is written, 'You shall worship the Lord your God, and Him only shall you serve' " (Matt. 4:10).

Although no outward relationship exists between Joseph's betrayals and the Lord's three temptations in the wilderness, in the deeper supreme sense both treat of the Lord's terrible temptations while on earth. Each in a sense is a summary of these trials. If we think about the emotions Joseph would have felt during his betrayals, we sense his inward agony. He begged his brothers not to betray him. He felt despair over the lies of Potiphar's wife, and then over his utterly unfair imprisonment. These betrayals picture the Lord's despair and agony in His temptations. This despair is *not* over His own fate. It is despair about His efforts to save the human race from evil. When the love is for others, and the despair is over the state of others, the resulting pain is incredible. Love and despair touch inner levels of the heart, beyond all outward trials.

Joseph in the pit and in prison is Jesus' love for our salvation trapped by the illusions instilled by the hells. They have Him imprisoned by the believable illusion that humankind is too evil to be saved. The Lord can clearly perceive the appalling nature of the evil in His own maternal heredity. He knows the states of evil in humankind. No wonder He despairs. It is such evils that led to the killing of six million Jews in Nazi concentration camps during World War II. It is such evils that lead to the betrayal of a husband or a wife by adultery. It is such evil that abuses children. The Lord sees the desire of the hells to destroy innocence on earth, to remove compassion from human hearts. They drive into the Lord's lower mind the illusion that they, the hells, will easily succeed.

This, in the supreme sense, is what Joseph's torments represent. While in the prison (in temptations) he interprets the butler's dream: the human senses (subject to the understanding) would be redeemed. But when so redeemed, they forget Joseph. There still remains a lack of connection between the senses in the Lord and His celestial human essence. Joseph remains in prison, forgotten.

The Word now tells (in Genesis 41) of Pharaoh's two dreams: first of seven fine-looking and fat cows that come up out of the river, and of seven other cows, ugly and gaunt, that eat up the fat cows. Then of seven good heads of grain being devoured by seven thin and blighted heads. These dreams deeply troubled Pharaoh, and he called all his magicians and wise men to interpret them. But "There was no one who could interpret them for Pharaoh" (Gen. 41:8). It was then at last that the chief butler remembered Joseph and his accurate interpretation of his dream and of the baker's. The butler told Pharaoh about the "Hebrew boy" (Gen. 41:12) who could truly interpret dreams.

"And Pharaoh sent for Joseph, and they hurried him out of the pit" (Gen. 41:14). What a change and rescue! Joseph had been in prison, seemingly to be forgotten until he died. Now, out of nowhere, he was raised up, his hair and beard were clipped, he was given fresh clothes and presented to the ruler of all Egypt.

What a liberating state this must have been in Jesus' life on earth! It is an uplifting and refreshing of the human essence after temptations and despair. This is an early prophecy of the Easter dawn, here a raising up from a state like death. This depicts a major and wonderful step in the glorification of His sensuous.

The human essence is elevated, released. Representatively, Pharaoh, who wished to have his dreams interpreted, does this.

Pharaoh represents the natural, here the natural in the broadest sense, which includes the ultimate or the sensuous level. Pharaoh in this context is said to represent "the new natural," which is ready now "to accept the celestial of the spiritual" (AC 5244), or Joseph. For us this means that the Lord comes directly to our sensuous level, bringing His love and light. Our sensuous level is beginning to respond to Him in open and free reception of His influx. With Jesus Himself this is a beginning of rebirth in the *will* of the sensuous, a beginning of the glorification on this ultimate and powerful level.

"And they hurried Joseph out of the pit" (Gen. 41:14).

Jesus' being in the pit is an entrapment by His finite human heredity. In the sphere of hereditary evil through this human, it seems that all hope for humankind is gone. Seeing the power and putrid nature of sensuous evils with humankind, Jesus must feel that we cannot be saved. The hells urge this illusion upon Him. But now, the devastating temptations are over. He is lifted up, into the clean and fresh air of Divine reality.

Imagine how the Lord feels here. He is lifted up from an agonizing temptation and restored to a state of Divine vision. He sees again that humankind can be saved, that it is open to salvation. He is filled with inmost joy (AC 2034).

Changes are coming then to the sensuous: the imagery is direct. **Joseph clipped his hair and beard.** The Lord is clipping away and casting aside that which was disheveled and in disorder in His sensuous. He becomes refreshed and appears in spiritual beauty. **Joseph discarded his worn and unclean prison apparel and put on fine garments** (AC 5248). **Joseph then came to Pharaoh,** which means that the love in Jesus opens up "communication with the new natural" (AC 5249).

Great changes are happening. Jesus is advancing in the glorification of His sensuous level to the point where the celestial of the spiritual now arises out of prison and becomes a leader, a profound interpreter of dreams. **Joseph stood before Pharaoh not as a former prisoner but as one who could tell the meaning of dreams and foretell the future.** Here is a hint of the full glorification that is to come, a hint of the Divine omniscience to come (AC 5249).

Pharaoh then unfolded to Joseph his two dreams about the fat and thin cows and the fat and thin heads of grain. Jehovah allowed Joseph to interpret them. Joseph's prophecy told of seven years of plenty followed by seven years of famine. He advised Pharaoh to store up grain during the good years to provide food for the bad ones that would follow.

In Pharaoh's eyes this prophecy and suggested plan were good. He asked, " 'Shall we find a man like this, in whom is the spirit of God?' And Pharaoh said to Joseph, 'After God has caused you to know all this, no one has wisdom and intelligence like you. You shall be over my house, and all my people shall kiss on your mouth; only in the throne will I be great, more than you. . . .See, I have set you over all the land of Egypt' " (Gen. 41:38-41).

Only hours before, Joseph had been in prison! Such is the power of celestial love in the human heart. After temptations, it rises to leadership, governing all the land of Egypt, all factual knowledges. For celestial love and the truth perceived from it are supreme in the human heart. They are the Lord with us. So also in the Lord's glorification: the Joseph in Him is raised up to leadership in His Egypt; the celestial rules in all the knowledges of creation.

"These events happened by Divine Providence so that Joseph might come to represent the celestial of the spiritual, which was the Lord's when He was in the world — the celestial of the spiritual being that by means of which the Lord exercised control over His natural and also His sensory awareness, so that step by step He could make both of these Divine" (AC 5316).

Pharaoh gave Joseph a new name, "Zaphenath Paneah" (Gen. 41:45), and gave him for a wife Asenath, the daughter of the priest of On. This name "Zaphenath Paneah" means "the essential nature of the celestial of the spiritual" (AC 5330), which is celestial love set in a foundation of spiritual truth.

The marriage of Joseph to Asenath indicates a higher and fuller union of good and truth within Jesus Christ, a marriage that enables the glorification to continue with power and fullness. But the essential nature of this marriage within the Lord is too deep and wonderful for human comprehension (AC 5332). It is a love of the tenderest kind, united now to a gentle, profound wisdom. It is the Lord coming nearer to us.

Chapter Thirty-Two

THE NEW WILL AND UNDERSTANDING IN THE SENSUOUS

JOSEPH'S EARLY RULE
GENESIS 41 CONTINUED

+ **As second ruler in Egypt, Joseph works for seven years to store up grain, preparing for the famine.**

+ **During this time, his wife bears two sons: Manasseh and Ephraim.**

+ **After seven years of plenty, the famine begins. The people of Egypt and of other lands come to Joseph to buy grain.**

"And Joseph was a son of thirty years when he stood before Pharaoh, king of Egypt" (Gen. 41:46). This age of thirty represents a state when "the quantity of remains was complete" (AC 5335). Jesus Christ on earth has endured many and severe temptations by the time He reaches the age of thirty. I believe that the Isaac rational is firmly established in Him by then, and also the glorified natural represented by Israel. Jesus must have been far advanced in His glorification to do the astonishing miracles of the next few years.

Pharaoh now appointed Joseph ruler. And Joseph went out "through all the land of Egypt. And in the seven years of abundance of corn the land yielded bunches. And Joseph gathered all the food of the seven years which were in the land of Egypt, and laid up the food in the cities. . . . And Joseph stored up grain like the sand of the sea, very much until he left off numbering, because it was beyond number" (Gen. 41:46-49, selections).

Within Jesus, the truths linked to good in His sensations are stored up in His "interior parts of the interior natural" (AC 5344). When He undergoes the seven years of famine, He has these stored-up Divine remains to draw upon. They carry Him with courage through the rest of His life on earth.

In us, these tremendous harvests of grain picture an advanced stage of rebirth when we become sensitive to the marvels, beauty, and interior miracles of nature. We sense new ways of helping others and new states of closeness in marriage. The Lord stores up these precious remains in the interior area of our mind. This is rich and full, just like the corn stored up in the cities of Egypt.

The Lord gives us these gifts for the difficult times we experience during the further rebirth of the sensuous that follows. He draws goods or loves out of these gifts to sustain us and to carry us through inner famine. By this process we are reborn. We see evils in order to shun them, and the Lord removes them. The Lord establishes this process in His own glorification of His sensuous mind (AC 5342:3). With Him, in His glorification in this state, the storing up of grain was **"like the sand of the sea, very much, until he left off numbering, because it was beyond number"** (Gen. **41:49**; see also AC 5346). Imagine the tremendous amount of good sensuous delights that move Jesus deeply – perhaps the beauty of nature and how good food serves human beings, the power of touch between a mother and child or a loving husband and wife, and many, many other delights. These things Jesus would store up to call upon later, during times when all would seem hopeless on the natural level of humanity.

". . .To Joseph were born two sons. . .whom Asenath the

daughter of Potipherah, the priest of On, bore to him. And Joseph called the name of the firstborn 'Manasseh – for God has made me forget all my labor and all my father's house.' And the name of the second he called 'Ephraim – for God has made me fruitful in the land of my affliction'" (Gen. 41: 50-52).

The birth of Manasseh and then Ephraim marks vital stages in the Lord's glorification. Manasseh symbolizes a new will within the Lord's sensuous (AC 5351). This brings a Divine spring and warmth that replace the coldness of evil through the finite maternal heredity. For the angels this is a time of joy, certainly a time when the songs of "Hallelujah" would ring in the heavens. For the Lord is coming to humankind in the most ultimate level of life (see CL 81).

In naming Manasseh, **Joseph said, "For God has made me forget all my toil, and all my father's house" (Gen. 41:51).** "The words 'For God has made me forget all my toil' mean 'the removal of the evils which have caused pain'" (AC 5352). Manasseh's inner promise for us is forgetfulness of evils that have plagued us all our lives. Now these evils leave central positions and go to the periphery of our consciousness where we forget them. It follows that when there is a new will in the sensuous, a new understanding will be born there also. This is the birth of Ephraim, who was named with the words: "God has made me fruitful in the land of my affliction" (Gen. 41:52). To be fruitful represents a multiplication of truths (AC 5356) in a new sensuous understanding.

But now the famine comes. What does this famine mean? Where the sensuous had felt the beginning of regeneration and lovely states of spring and summer opening up the heart, there now comes a change. A late autumn and winter come to the heart, desolation in the spirit, a void or emptying out. Delight seems to disappear for us, including delights of the senses. Things seem empty, purposeless (AC 5360). Fortunately, in this inner famine we do not die in our spirits; **there is grain stored up in the cities of Egypt.** If we go to Joseph, to our inmost love, we can draw out memories of remains that sustain us, but just barely. We are poignantly aware of a famine, an emptiness, all around us within our minds.

The Lord helps to explain what is going on spiritually in rebirth.

"With those who are being regenerated. . .truths are multiplied exceedingly; for these people have an affection for knowing truths. But as they draw nearer to the point when their regeneration is actually carried out, they are seemingly deprived of those truths. For those truths are withdrawn to a more interior position, and when this happens, the person seems to experience desolation. Nevertheless those truths are returned in consecutive stages to the natural (sensuous here), where they are joined to good while the person is being regenerated. . . .The desolation. . .is meant by the famine lasting for seven years" (AC 5376:2).

The Lord permits this desolation because only in this state do the evils and falsities that lie concealed in the sensuous emerge to be seen for what they are. Then, drawing on the remains stored up in the interiors of our minds, the Lord can help us fight against and shun those now evident evils. We see what is blocking us off from heavenly states.

To encourage us in this process, the Lord tells us in the Writings: "Desolation occurs to the end that a person may be regenerated, that is, to the end that evils and falsities may first be separated from him, and then truths may be joined to forms of good, and forms of good to truths" (AC 5376:7).

"Jehovah will comfort Zion, He will comfort all her waste places, so much so that He will make her wilderness like Eden, and her desert like the garden of Jehovah. Gladness and joy will be found in her, confession and the voice of song" (Isaiah 51:3).

Chapter Thirty-Three

THE SENSUOUS RESPONDS TO A NEW ORDER

THE TEN SONS OF JACOB GO TO EGYPT
GENESIS 42

+ Back in Canaan, Jacob sends his ten older sons to Egypt to buy grain.

+ Joseph recognizes his brothers, but they do not recognize him. Joseph conceals his identity and speaks roughly to them.

+ The ten brothers believe they are suffering because of their cruel treatment of Joseph. In private, Joseph weeps over their remorse.

+ Joseph holds Simeon hostage while the nine other brothers return to Canaan with grain. Joseph commands them to return with their youngest brother, Benjamin. In secret, he returns their money into the sacks of grain that they have bought.

Learning that there was food in Egypt during the terrible famine, Jacob sent Joseph's ten brothers down to buy grain. Benjamin, his beloved youngest son, he kept behind. He did not want to lose Benjamin, as he had lost Joseph.

The ten brothers arrived in Egypt, and "Joseph's brothers

came and bowed down to him, faces to the earth. . . .And Joseph recognized his brothers, and they did not recognize him. And Joseph remembered the dreams which he had dreamed involving them" (Gen. 42:6-9, selections).

Joseph spoke hard words to them, calling them spies. This they denied, saying they had come to buy food and that they were all sons of one man in the land of Canaan. "And behold the youngest is with our father today, and one is not" (Gen. 42:13).

But Joseph tested them, telling them that they should choose one to go and fetch their brother in Canaan, and that he would keep the rest in bonds in Egypt. "Bring your youngest brother to me, and your words will be verified and you will not die" (Gen. 42:20).

And they said. . ."Assuredly we are guilty concerning our brother, whose anguish of soul we saw when he pleaded with us, and we did not hear; therefore this anguish has come to us" (Gen. 42:21).

"Joseph turned away from them, and wept; and he came back to them and spoke to them; and he took Simeon from them, and bound him before their eyes. And Joseph gave command to fill their vessels with grain, and to restore their silver, each man's in his sack. . ." (Gen. 42:24,25).

Joseph is the Lord's human essence on earth, not yet glorified. He now sees in His sensuous nature, which had been flawed with hereditary evil through a finite human mother, the beginning of a change. Joseph's two sons symbolize this beginning. Now Joseph saw his brothers experiencing guilt over their earlier betrayal of him; he could see their genuine anguish. He could not help weeping.

The same is true of the Lord on earth when He sees the beginning of true glorification in His sensuous level. It may be said that Jesus weeps, as indeed it is twice recorded of Him in the New Testament. This change in Himself, this glorification of His sensuous, would make possible almost incredible future changes for humankind on earth. Joseph wept; that is, the Lord weeps. This is celestial love crying — here out of *joy*.

But there is still much to be accomplished in the full glorification of this lowest level. **Benjamin was not yet reunited with Joseph, nor was Jacob.** Spiritually, these are the missing keys. **Joseph did not imprison all the brothers. Rather, he bound only Simeon, sending the others back to Jacob. So the nine brothers began their journey back home.**

Early in this return journey, one of them opened his sack and found that the silver they had paid for grain had been mysteriously restored to them. "And they trembled, saying a man to his brother, 'What is this that God has done to us?" (Gen. 42:28). They came to Jacob and told him all that had happened: that Simeon remained bound in Egypt and that this unknown ruler demanded that Benjamin be brought down to him.

"And Jacob their father said to them, 'You have bereaved me; Joseph is not, and Simeon is not, and you take Benjamin'. . . .And Jacob said, 'My son shall not go down with you, for his brother is dead, and he, he alone, is left. And should harm happen to him on the road in which you go, you will cause my grey hair to go down in sorrow to the grave' " (Gen. 42:36,38).

The attempts by Joseph's brothers to procure any more grain without bringing their youngest brother Benjamin down to Egypt would be futile. In the celestial and spiritual senses, Benjamin must be in Egypt, and finally Joseph must be seen and acknowledged by his brothers as the true ruler. Celestial love (Joseph) and living truth (Benjamin) must be present before anything genuine (grain) can be taken from knowledges (Egypt) (AC 5396, 5397).

Without such love and truth present, there is the attempt to reason one's way from the senses up to Divine truth. Ishmael, the wild-ass rational, is the first to represent this attempt in adult life. Now, many years later, human beings in advanced rebirth attempt to find truth on the sensuous level by reasoning their way upward from science and from the senses. But this cannot be done (AC 5397). Truth on any level always comes from above, from heavenly love, through perception (AC 6047). Truth does not come from below, from the senses alone. Missing here is not only a known and recognized Joseph, but also and especially Benjamin.

Benjamin is the "spiritual of the celestial," or truth coming from celestial good. He is a go-between, between higher and lower qualities, between the celestial represented by Joseph, and the natural and sensuous represented by the other ten sons of Jacob. As a medium, he is said to draw qualities from each: from the celestial and from the natural.

As we have seen, the nine sons told their father what had happened to them in Egypt, how the ruler had demanded that Benjamin be brought down to him and had kept Simeon bound in ransom. They told Jacob Joseph's words to them: ". . .Bring your youngest brother to me, and I shall know that you are not spies, that you are upright men; I will give you your brother (Simeon), and you will wander through the land, trading" (Gen. 42:33,34). Joseph said, in effect: Bring Benjamin down to me in Egypt and you will become successful traders.

If Benjamin is present and all twelve sons of Jacob are then in Egypt together with Joseph as ruler, wonderful things will happen. The sons will flourish and grow in bounty as successful "traders." What is pictured here spiritually is the goal of rebirth in the sensuous for us, and the goal for the Lord, the path establisher, in the glorification of His sensuous. This goal is that Joseph, or inmost love, should rule in the human heart, even at the lowest levels.

This rule is one of tender, unselfish love. Joined to it are living and sparkling truths, represented by Benjamin's presence. When these two are both present in the interior levels of our mind, the external truths of the sensuous, represented by the other ten sons of

Jacob, assume true and heavenly order. Willingly and lovingly subordinate to Joseph, as he had dreamed long before at the age of seventeen, they do not become slaves, but rather alive and free. They successfully trade in wonderful goods and truths in the sensuous level of life. The lowest level of our being becomes heavenly, responsive, and receptive of inmost love (see AC 5227).

With the glorified Lord, this is the Divine order from which all human order flows. The Divine celestial, love itself, governs in creation and human hearts, and Divine truths from this provide the means for this to happen. Then all lower truths serve willingly and also become alive and Divine. This is the goal in His glorification.

However, Jacob, representing a higher good within the natural, feels he cannot survive without Benjamin. When there is disorder on a lower plane, the plane right above it is in obscurity and confusion. This good within the natural (Jacob), cannot see the full picture; it does not know that Joseph is alive and ruling in Egypt and that if Benjamin joins him, then wonderful things will happen. This would include, eventually, a reunion of Jacob himself with his whole family in Egypt. But especially this would focus on Jacob's reunion with Joseph, his beloved son, who he thinks is dead.

We cannot foresee the miracles the Lord has in store for us. The despair in us blinds our eyes. Shakespeare wrote, "We know what we are, but we know not what we may be" (*Hamlet*, Act 4, Scene 5).

Jacob, viewing things from his present perspective, despairs. In the spiritual sense this expresses the despair of goodness in the natural (Jacob or Israel) if deprived of the only internal level it now possesses (Benjamin, or inner truth from love). The inmost love from infancy (Joseph) is gone, apparently dead. **Benjamin had taken Joseph's place in Jacob's heart. And now he feared losing Benjamin: "And should harm happen to him on the road on which you go, you will cause my grey hair to go down in sorrow to the grave" (Gen. 42:38).**

Spiritually, Jacob or good in the natural is saying, "If inner truth from good is lost to me, then this will be the 'final phase of the church' (AC 5550) in me." "Grey hair," means this final phase (*Ibid.*). " 'In sorrow to the grave' means without hope of a restoration to life" (AC 5551). As is so often true of us, Jacob sees only his immediate circumstances. Without such inner truths (Benjamin) in this state, we feel we are only animals, which will die and be buried. There will be no life after death.

To be without hope is devastating. That is how Jacob felt about losing Benjamin, and so we feel if we are without truth that is alive. Yet an astonishing surprise is coming for Jacob. The Lord promises this for us as well if we patiently follow the path of life.

Chapter Thirty-Four

"NEW" TRUTHS COME TO CELESTIAL LOVE

BENJAMIN COMES TO JOSEPH
GENESIS 43

> ✦ When their purchased grain runs out, Israel (Jacob) tells his sons to travel to Egypt to buy more. Judah reminds him that they have been commanded to bring Benjamin with them.

> ✦ With great sadness, Israel agrees, and all the brothers leave for Egypt.

> ✦ Joseph greets them warmly, and prepares a feast for them.

Genesis 43 begins, **"And the famine grew more serious in the land" (Gen. 43:1).** The first thing said in a series is often the key to all that follows. "Famine" represents an absence of good — a state of desolation.

During the Lord's process of glorifying His sensuous level, His finite or maternal human heredity is resistant and very active. It blocks the influx of Divine good into the Lord's lowest mind. In this sensuous level He feels desolation, a lack of hope for the salvation of humankind.

But this chapter brings a refreshing change. One of the key

elements missing in the Lord's human essence is now brought directly to Him where it can help restore joy and begin to push away this desolation. **Benjamin was brought down to Egypt and into the presence of his long-lost brother Joseph. The famine had become so desperate in Canaan that Israel had to yield up his youngest son to accompany his nine brothers down to Egypt. As Judah urged so strongly, only in this way would the ruler in Egypt receive them, for that ruler had demanded that Benjamin be brought down. Heartsick at this, Israel nevertheless had to give in. It was good that he did, for it changed his life.**

In a first brief meeting with his ten brothers in Egypt, Joseph saw that, at last, Benjamin was with them. He ordered a special feast and released Simeon from being held hostage. At last they all came fully into Joseph's presence at a feast of first reunion. But it was only a first or preliminary reunion: the eleven brothers still had no idea that the ruler was actually Joseph. In their minds, Joseph was dead.

Although Benjamin saw Joseph with his own eyes, he, too, had no idea this was his closest brother.

"And Joseph came to the house, and they [the eleven brothers] brought him the gift that was in their hand, to the house, and bowed down to Joseph to the earth" (Gen. 43:26).

This again harks back to Joseph's dream at age seventeen. Only his father and mother were still missing. Joseph asked his brothers if their father "had peace? Is he still alive?" (Gen. 43:27). They replied that he was.

"And Joseph lifted up his eyes, and saw Benjamin his brother, his mother's son, and said, 'Is this your youngest brother, whom you said [something about] to me?' And he said, 'God be gracious to you, my son.' And Joseph hastened, because feelings of compassion were being roused in him toward his brother, and he sought [somewhere] to weep, and he went into his bed

chamber and wept there" (Gen. 43:30). Benjamin was his closest brother; he and Benjamin alone shared Rachel as mother.

Divinely this is a first reunion within Jesus in His human essence, one that He sought for a very long time. His heart has yearned for the truth that is symbolized by Benjamin. At this time the inmost in the Lord's finite human essence is celestial — the celestial that is a pure love of the human race. But this celestial love has lacked its partner, its brother, which is the living, sparkling truth that comes from the celestial. Now it is brought to Him in a reunion that advances His glorification wonderfully. The emotion expressed by Joseph when he sees Benjamin discloses Jesus' feelings at this time.

The Lord felt a "mercy springing out of love" (AC 5691). "When such mercy bursts forth it does so from what is inmost, and it does so as fast as the blink of an eye or flash of an idea" (AC 5690). It is said, "feelings of compassion were being roused in Joseph" (Gen. 43:30). "In the original language, 'feelings of compassion' is expressed by a word which describes inmost or most tender love" (AC 5691).

That love is what the celestial level feels when it is united with the spiritual truth that clearly expresses its nature. It feels wholeness, a oneness. With Jesus Christ this is deeply moving. Prior to this, the human essence has been conjoined with the wonderful but limited truth of the angels in the heavens. But now the Divine Truth itself is near – the clear, complete, and Divinely true way of seeing and understanding all things of life. This truth is superior to that seen by any of the celestial angels of the Most Ancient heavens. Step by step the "Human Divine", or the angels who had mediated for Jehovah, are being replaced by the Divine Human of Jesus, and this even on the sensuous level (AC 5663:3). This process is only in an early stage; it was like a "general influx before the joining together" (AC 5574). But it evokes tenderest love in Jesus, because it heralds what is to come when His work on earth is complete.

The process by which Joseph revealed himself to his brothers also tells of the gradual unifying of our spiritual being — of our becoming "one" before the Lord, our becoming little children in His eyes. It speaks of a coming into wisdom that is filled with innocence and trust. This is possible for us because the Lord Incarnate undergoes these advanced stages in His glorification. The Joseph in Him is gradually revealed to His lower mind as it is purified of His finite maternal heredity.

". . .The Word became flesh and dwelt among us, and we beheld His glory, the glory as of the only begotten of the Father, full of grace and truth" (John 1:14). Benjamin is Divine truth, "full of grace." The Lord in His human essence, before He is glorified, receives this Divine truth finitely but deeply. More and more, this truth in Him becomes Divine; it is glorified (AC 10053; see AC 9315, 9198).

These inmost truths speak directly of why the Lord made us, why we were born, what our inmost destiny is in His eyes. The story of the reunion of Joseph, Benjamin, and Israel speaks directly to the human heart.

At some point in our lives we learn from the Word that all good and truth is really the Lord's, and that *of ourselves* we do not have a good heavenly self. Part of us rebels against this. If all of our good is from the Lord, what is ours? People who are good have a state in which they "make the existence of a separate selfhood vital to delight" (AC 5660:2). The Lord doesn't break this state. He allows us to go on with our own thinking even to the point of almost deciding we don't want good and truth if they come only from the Lord. At first we don't feel enough selfhood in this, and therefore we are allowed to try to find good and truth from some other source.

The Lord allows us the freedom to search and search until we realize that there is no other source, and come freely to accept His leadership in our hearts (AC 5660:2).

The Lord is now giving or offering us a "new will" (AC

5660:3). This is a heavenly selfhood, and those who receive it "no longer see only themselves in every single thing they do or in every single thing they learn about and convey to others. Instead they see their neighbor, the general public, the Church, the Lord's kingdom, and so the Lord Himself. The ends (or purposes) they have in life are what undergo change; for ends which have lower things — namely self and the world — in view are removed and higher ones are introduced to replace them" (AC 5660:3).

We *are* the ends or purposes we have in view. Our ends speak of the things we love the most, of what we want to accomplish or be. In the process of rebirth, a person becomes unselfish goals or loves! The Lord alone can do this. He alone can make an angel. What is it like to experience this change?

"The person who is given a heavenly selfhood enjoys. . .a state of serenity and peace, for he trusts in the Lord and believes that no evil at all can come to touch him, knowing too that no strong evil desire can molest him. More than that, those who have received a heavenly selfhood enjoy true freedom, for being led by the Lord constitutes freedom, since one is then led within the sphere of good, from good, and to good. From this it becomes clear that they enjoy bliss and happiness, for nothing exists to disturb them — no self-love at all, consequently no enmity, hatred or vengeance at all; nor any love of the world at all, consequently no deceitfulness, fear or unease at all" (AC 5660:3).

We find a hint of this oncoming state in the last verses of Genesis 43, which speak of the happy feast Joseph gave for his eleven brothers. What a fulfillment this was to Joseph. He knew who these eleven men were, and his heart sang. He felt something of the release spoken of that comes with a "heavenly self-hood"! **But this would have been like only a prophecy, for the eleven brothers did not know who Joseph was. There was no**

reciprocal joy yet in their hearts, only a wonder and trepidation. Representatively, evils were still present in the external natural level (represented by the ten brothers) that prohibited Joseph from revealing who he truly was.

Chapter Thirty-Five

TEMPTATIONS TO SPIRITUAL THEFT

THE SILVER CUP
GENESIS 44

+ Joseph fills his brother's sacks with grain. Secretly, he places their money back into the sacks, and his own silver cup into Benjamin's sack.

+ When the brothers have left, Joseph sends his servant to pursue them, and accuses them of stealing his cup.

+ Joseph says he will keep Benjamin as a slave, and the rest may go free.

+ In desperation, Judah offers himself as a slave instead, explaining that their father may die if they do not bring Benjamin back.

The story now centers on Joseph's silver cup, and is spiritually about temptations that are frighteningly intense. **Joseph commanded that the pouches of the eleven brothers be filled with food, "as much as they can carry; and put each one's silver in the mouth of his pouch. And you are to put my cup, the cup made of silver, in the mouth of the pouch of the youngest, and his silver for grain" (Gen. 44:1,2). Joseph was speaking to his chief servant, giving these instructions. The servant complied,**

and when morning dawned, the eleven were sent away.

They were only a little beyond the city when Joseph commanded his chief servant to pursue the eleven and accuse them of stealing his silver cup. The servant overtook them and accused them of theft. They strongly denied this and said, "With whomever of your servants the cup is found, let him die; and we also will be slaves of my lord. . . .And he [the chief servant] searched; he began with the oldest and finished with the youngest. And the cup was found in Benjamin's pouch. And they rent their clothes; and each one loaded his ass, and they returned to the city" (Gen. 44:9,12,13). They came back in despair.

The brothers then came before Joseph, "and fell before him to the earth" (Gen. 44:14). They made no excuses even though literally they had not stolen. They simply said, "We are my lord's slaves, even ourselves, even he in whose hand the cup was found" (Gen. 44:16). Joseph said no, only Benjamin would be his slave. Then Judah made his plea. He told what he had promised his father Israel before taking Benjamin away from Canaan to Egypt. Judah said that if Benjamin did not return now, it would kill their father. "And now I beg you, let your servant stay instead of the boy, a slave to my lord, and let the boy go up with his brothers" (Gen. 44: 33).

This was Judah speaking, who had originally sold Joseph into Egypt for money. What a change had come upon him! Seeing this willingness to sacrifice himself in Judah, Joseph could not contain his love and compassion. Genesis 45 describes the touching reunion that then openly took place.

These temptations focused on theft, on the proclivity of the Lord's finite maternal human to steal what was rightfully Divine. Theft is so inscribed on hereditary evil that it seems impossible to eradicate it. It is deep and fundamental to the states of mediate good within us, in which we take much credit for things. However, it *is* an evil, and in time it must be seen as such and shunned if we are ever to become free.

The apparent theft of Joseph's cup does not represent the Lord's last temptations directly. These come later, at the very end of Genesis. Nevertheless, on the cross the Lord's finite maternal human would have cried out for its own self-life, the cry of that innate urge for self-preservation that is written on our very bodies. "My God, My God, why have You forsaken Me?" (Matt. 27:46) But the Lord, at the very end, gave up the illusion of self-life held by His finite sensuous level, inherited through Mary. He broke that illusion: "Father, into Your hands I commend My spirit" (Luke 23:46).

This final state has not yet come upon Jesus. The apparent theft of Joseph's cup is a powerful temptation that comes before His final ones. It may have involved the Lord's seeing in His finite human how merit is inscribed on human hearts. The despair He feels is for us: how can human beings ever be freed of this evil that they hug to themselves so tightly for warmth? His despair is crushing. Yet He does not yield. He sees the possibility of rebirth even on the lowest level of the love of self. For in the end, did not Judah offer himself as a slave to Joseph, even as the lowest or sensuous love of self can be reborn and submit to the celestial in our hearts?

Joseph's silver cup evokes images in our memories. One thinks of the Holy Grail, which legend has it was used by Jesus at the Last Supper and was brought to Britain, where it was often sought. Every time we take the Holy Supper, we drink from a cup, often a silver cup. The correspondence of Joseph's silver cup is vital in our spiritual lives, for it represents truth seen powerfully and as living reality itself. The silver cup is truth seen beyond any doubt, even as angels perceive truths in heaven. We seek this cup!

Joseph, the celestial within us, fills the spiritual level (Benjamin) with perceptions of truths — truths that are alive, that are the only truths of the true church! They are called this because they alone are truly living for us. Here is one of life's beautiful states: when truths in us receive loves that inflow from our very inmost, from our earliest childhood innocence and remains, and these truths become alive. They are like wine in the silver cup (AC 5728) and like the new wine at the wedding feast at Cana.

But such a wonderful state is abhorrent to the hells, and especially to the hells who tempt Jesus Christ when the internal celestial is flowing powerfully into the intermediary with Him, causing that intermediary (Benjamin) to bring the very Divine present with it (AC 5689:2). This is the new state coming upon Jesus Christ: He is becoming the Divine truth — the "Word made flesh" (John 1:14). This level in the Lord is not yet Divine, but its quality is "next to the Divine" (AC 5689).

This major progress in the glorification is greeted with venom and hatred by the hells. They know what is happening, sensing it through their presence in the Lord's finite maternal heredity. Seeing this new progress in Jesus, they attack with all the malice they possess. So it is with us, after we have experienced the silver cup, and have fully known its marvel. The hells will attack, and this is our opportunity to make this new state permanent, from the Lord's power.

These temptations are of our sensuous plane. They persist until there is willing submission of this lowest level to the internal celestial (see AC 5729).

Despair is life's hardest state to endure. Despair is a loss of hope. All joy in life has hope within it. In this temptation with us, the evil within our sensuous feels that it has been discovered, exposed. *It* is giving up its hope, and that wracks the human heart. With the Lord, as we have said, it is despair about human beings ever overcoming spiritual theft — despair instilled through the Lord's maternal human.

The despair is expressed in the literal story by the reaction of the brothers when Joseph's chief servant finds the silver cup

in Benjamin's pouch. They must have felt, "What's the use?" They tore their clothes in misery, and as we have already seen, went back to Joseph and fell down to the earth in front of him. They said, "God has found out the iniquity of your servants" (Gen. 44:16), and we and Benjamin are your slaves. They knew that they had been dishonest to Jacob in the past even though in this instance they had not themselves stolen. When Joseph said no, he would keep Benjamin only, then Judah offered himself instead, and he meant it with all his heart. These brothers felt utter despair.

This is not only a spiritual story of temptation but also an illustration of the uses that can come out of such difficult permissions. What evil is surfacing for open acknowledgment and the opportunity for shunning? The Writings respond:

"The whole of this chapter has as its subject spiritual theft, which consists in laying claim to good and truth that come from the Lord. This is a matter of consequence so great that after death a person cannot be admitted into heaven until he acknowledges in his heart that nothing good or true originates in himself, only in the Lord, and that whatever originates in himself is nothing but evil.

"The truth of this is proved to a person after death by means of many experiences. . . .Laying claim therefore to truth or good as one's own is the opposite of the attitude of mind that reigns universally in heaven. It is the opposite of the acknowledgment that all salvation is due to mercy" (AC 5758:1,2).

These words are easy to accept in theory. It is not hard to say that all good and truth are the Lord's. But to really acknowledge this is a lifelong struggle, a struggle that intensifies in the advanced regeneration of human beings and the advanced glorification of the Lord. How many of our daily motivations are based on wanting to appear intelligent or sharp or wise? How often are we concerned about our position, our superiority? How often do we think we are good because we have done this or that? This common human trait is termed "self-righteousness" in the Word, and it is said that from this quality "many evils well up. Thinking in this way, a person sees himself in every specific deed he performs for his neighbor; and when he does this he loves himself more than anyone else" (*Ibid.*).

The feeling of merit is terribly hard to get rid of; it has its own secret warmth, warmth that can hold us in bondage and limit our lives.

The silver cup in Benjamin's pouch speaks of this merit, this theft. Here the merit is especially over truth — thinking of truth as our own, not the Lord's. Prior to advanced regeneration, the lower level in us insists on taking credit for the truth it sees. It is interesting that in the literal story the **ten brothers admitted guilt for the theft, when in this case they had not actually stolen (Gen. 44: 16)**! Here the spiritual reality overrides the literal situation (AC 5747:2). Yet the ten had been dishonest in the past, and therefore a literal truth exists as well.

Spiritually, the theft is actual. Their guilt about this is completely valid. Spiritually, our lower level has been stealing from the Lord for years without our feeling any shame or guilt. We are happy to claim credit for the wonderful truths we know and speak about. Suddenly we awaken spiritually. The highest and most innocent level in us (Joseph) accuses us of stealing from the Lord, and now we know this is true. When and if we actually feel this in our hearts, we despair about ourselves. How despicable we are at this level! How can we ever change? Our despair is complete, even as it was with the ten brothers who offered themselves to Joseph as slaves.

Judah offered himself in place of Benjamin. Earlier, Judah represented love of self in the lower level of our hearts and minds, but now this evil self-love is being shunned, to be replaced by an orderly self-love that looks to the Lord. This new love of self (the new Judah) at last sees the real guilt of the former love and submits itself completely to what is inmost, which in reality contains the Lord

Himself. A real regeneration is taking place here, and it comes about only through first experiencing despair. The sensuous in us is truly becoming subordinate.

One of the vital factors that enables this change to happen is that spiritually Benjamin is now present with Joseph. Benjamin represents a new perception of truths that was not there before. This perception, when joined with the celestial love (Joseph), enables us to shun what before we could not shun. Because we now see truth as living from the Lord, and see it from highest love, we can therefore shun any taking of merit by our outer self. The Lord can purge this level of its conceit. Truth of a higher level cleanses goods on a lower level, and this *is* the heavenly marriage while we are regenerating. This higher truth is Benjamin, and he has vision because of our spiritual Joseph.

The silver cup was in Benjamin's sack. But in the end, instead of this being a theft, Benjamin's possession of the cup was a true and wonderful representation. The silver cup, the grail, *is* his! The last thing he would do is to take merit for it! For he is the Lord active in the truth we now see and love.

Benjamin has been called "a child of Israel's old age, the youngest one" (Gen. 44:20). The meaning of "old age" is "newness of life" (AC 5804), and "a child of his old age, the youngest one" means "truth that is new" (*Ibid.*). Now there are perceptions of truth that a person "did not and could not know previously" (*Ibid.*). This applies both to Jesus at this stage, and to each one of us at this stage. Now truths possess "life," whereas before they had "little life in them" (*Ibid.*).

Benjamin, when he is with his father Israel, depicts truth seen from spiritual good, and this is called "new truth" (AC 5806). This is because truth seen from a state of goodness is the only truth that is living. We see it as reality itself.

But Benjamin represents a deeper insight into truth when he is with Joseph. Then he is said to represent "truth even more interior"

(*Ibid.*). Truth springing from celestial love (Joseph) is from an even higher level. Celestial good is higher than spiritual good. Love of the neighbor (Israel) or spiritual love is a wonderful love, and it brings warm and beautiful insights. But love of the Lord or celestial love brings warmth and light and visions of use that are higher even than insights from love of the neighbor.

With the Lord in His glorification, this "new truth" is Divine truth drawing near; it represents the Lord's *becoming Divine Truth* by degrees. The Joseph quality within Jesus Christ brings Him a nearness to His Soul, and explains Jesus' teachings and ministry during the last three years of His life on earth. It would explain the miracles He did that restored not only broken bodies, but also broken spiritual hearts, and even life itself. The inmost origin of such miracles is His Divine Soul.

Speaking of human beings, we would note that the Joseph or celestial "good is like a little flame, which sheds light and provides illumination, and so enables a person to see, perceive and believe truths" (AC 5816:2). Then these inner truths, now alive (Benjamin), can order and subordinate truths in our lower mind. Thus Benjamin is the link, the intermediate, that allows our *whole mind* to become alive to mercy and to love. With Benjamin present, the Lord's mercy can inflow from the inmost, through truths seen from that inmost, and then down to our outer mind and senses. This mercy of the Lord makes us alive spiritually (see AC 5816, 5822).

The key to having this happen is shunning evils in the sensuous level of our lives. Good cannot flow in and reveal itself while evils still occupy this level. This chapter, with the brothers' despair and their full submission in freedom, speaks more deeply of shunning evils in our outermost life. We are asked by the Lord to cleanse our sensuous thinking from lusts and sense addictions. What is more difficult? But the result will be the coming of the Lord.

Chapter Thirty-Six

CELESTIAL LOVE REVEALED

JOSEPH REVEALS HIS IDENTITY
GENESIS 45

+ With great tenderness, Joseph now reveals his
identity to his astonished brothers. He urges them to
go and fetch their father and their wives and
children, and to come and live in Egypt with him.

"And Joseph could not contain himself before all those
standing with him; and he cried out, 'Make every man go out
from me.' And no one stood with him while Joseph made himself known to his brothers. And he gave forth his voice in weeping, and the Egyptians heard, and the house of Pharaoh heard.
And Joseph said, 'I am Joseph. Is my father still alive?' And his
brothers could not answer him, for they were filled with dismay
at his presence" (Gen. 45:3).

After all, this was the brother they had betrayed, the brother they had wished to kill. Now Joseph asked them to draw near
him, and he talked with them from his heart:

"Do not be grieved, and do not have anger in your eyes that

you sold me here; for God sent me before you for the bestowal of life. . . .God sent me before you to establish for you a remnant on the earth, and for the bestowal of life on you for a great escape. And now you did not send me here, but God. . . .Make haste and go up to my father, and say to him, 'Thus said your son Joseph: God has established me as the lord for all Egypt; come down to me, do not delay. And you shall dwell in the land of Goshen. . . .And I will sustain you there, for there are still five years of famine'. . . .And behold, your eyes see, and the eyes of my brother Benjamin, that with my mouth I am speaking to you. . . .

" 'And you must tell my father about all my glory in Egypt, and all that you see; and you must make haste, and cause my father to come down here.' And Joseph fell on the neck of Benjamin his brother, and wept, and Benjamin wept on his neck. And he kissed all his brothers, and wept on them; and after that his brothers talked with him" (Gen. 45: selections).

This family that had been torn in two was reunited. Joseph, who had been considered dead, was found alive. Celestial love, which comes from remains and innocence from infancy, has long been hidden. Now rebirth is advanced far enough for this love to reveal itself again in the consciousness of our hearts. We thought the innocent joys of infancy were dead, but now we see and *feel* that they are alive.

Joseph said, "God sent me. . . .for the bestowal of life on you for a great escape" (Gen. 45:7). Escape from what? From hell, from being eternally in hell. Many of us may have a deep fear of going to hell, for something in us feels we deserve it, and at the same time we are afraid of this damnation. But Joseph now reveals that he is sent before us for a great escape. The remains of earliest infancy are the counterbalance to all our hereditary evil. And if as adults we try to shun evils as best we can with the Lord's help, then the Joseph in us will deliver us from bondage and lead us to a "great

214

escape." Joseph is the Lord's gift to each human heart, a gift waiting to be received.

The affections expressed in this part of Genesis are a revelation of Divine love. Few stories in the Word have the tenderness of this chapter. Inmostly, Joseph symbolizes the Lord. Here the Lord reveals Who He is: celestial love that embraces living truth (Benjamin) and integrates the entire human mind.

With the Lord Himself, in His glorification, Joseph's revelation of his identity is a high point of His being glorified. It speaks of the long-sought uniting of celestial good and spiritual truth within Him. **Joseph and Benjamin embraced each other, and wept for joy.** This love and truth in the human essence, next to the Divine, pave the way for the full glorification that is soon to come. Divine truth is now integrated within the Lord's Human. He has *become* Divine truth: "the Word became flesh" (John 1:14; see also AC 4538, 9670, 9199, 9315). He will become, stage by stage, the Divine good: Jesus Christ glorified.

All that is needed now is for Israel, the father, to join them. Israel will be sent for, and when he comes down he can see with his own eyes and feel with his heart the reality that Joseph is alive. Joseph said to his brothers: "Tell my father [Israel] about all my glory in Egypt" (Gen. 45: 13). This is not Joseph being prideful; it is rather Joseph speaking out of love, reassuring his father that all is well. The words, "Tell my father about all my glory" give a key to what this revelation of Joseph may be in the New Testament, in the Lord's own life on earth.

When, in the New Testament prior to the Easter story, does the Lord Jesus Christ first clearly show Who He is? When does He show His glory and deeply move the disciples who were with Him?

"Now after six days Jesus took Peter, James, and John his brother, and brought them up on a high mountain by themselves, and was transfigured before them. His face shone like the sun, and

His clothes were as white as light. And behold, Moses and Elijah appeared to them, talking with Him. Then Peter answered and said to Jesus, 'Lord, it is good for us to be here' " (Matt. 17:1-4).

If Joseph's manifestation of who he was parallels the Lord's transfiguration, then each of these stories casts light on the other. This is especially so in the celestial and spiritual senses of the Word (AC 5922).

On the mount of transfiguration the Lord shows Peter, James, and John His glory. He shows them "what His Divine Human was like, and what it looked like in Divine light" (AC 5922:5). They are seeing the Lord in His Divinity for the first time. It prepares them for the Lord's very last temptations and for the beautiful victory of Easter morning. Easter night, they see the Lord in His Divine Human, when He appears in their midst.

Joseph showed his glory to his brothers and he did so out of love. At the mount of transfiguration, the Lord shows His glory to the three disciples; He shows that He is the ruler not only of Egypt (the sciences), but also of the universe. At the transfiguration the Lord reveals that He is the Divine truth, and reveals the glory of this. Joseph with Benjamin represents the Divine truth that comes from Divine love. This is a pre-vision, a prophecy, of the complete glorification.

The open uniting of Joseph with his brothers symbolizes the actual joining together of the internal and external loves within us (see AC 5867). Loves make up our life, and now there are heavenly loves with both our inner and our sensuous levels.

This union, though beautiful, lacks a key presence. To make the picture complete, Israel the father must come down to Goshen to join his family. Even Pharaoh was aware of this key absence. He said to Joseph:

"Say to your brothers, 'Do this: Load your animals and go, get you to the land of Canaan. And take your father and your

**households, and come to me'. . . .And Joseph sent his brothers
away, and they went; and Joseph said to them, 'Do not quarrel
on the way.' And they went up out of Egypt, and came to the
land of Canaan, to Jacob their father. And they told him saying,
'Joseph is alive, and he has dominion in all the land of Egypt.'
And Jacob's heart failed, for he did not believe them. And they
spoke to him all of Joseph's words which he had spoken to
them, and he saw the carts which Joseph had sent to carry him,
and the spirit of Jacob revived. And Israel said, 'Enough;
Joseph my son is still alive. I will go and see him before I die' "
(Gen. 45:17,18,24-28).**

"[It is] enough!" This understates the surging joy in Israel.
Israel has taken on a newer representation than earlier in this spiritual history, when Jacob's change to Israel represented the regeneration or rebirth of the natural level of our mind. Now Israel is goodness in general in our natural lives. This goodness must come and
be united with Joseph, Benjamin, and the ten brothers. For then the
human mind is regenerate on all its levels, and the mind and heart
stand complete: an angel before the Lord.

Our inmost celestial remains or loves need the sparkling truths
represented by Benjamin in order to purify our outer sensations and
reactions (the ten brothers). And a part of this picture is spiritual
love, or charity, which Israel represents. Charity, spiritual goodness
active in our natural lives, is a key to genuine religion. "All religion
is of the life, and the life of religion is to do that which is good"
(Life 1).

Genuine charity brings all levels of our mind and heart together. Only what we *do* for others out of genuine and sincere motives
really brings heaven to us. This unites our inmost remains and the
truths we love with all our outer life. It brings fulfillment. **As Israel
said: "[It is] enough!"**

**It is vital that Israel come down and join all his family in
Egypt.** This represents Divine good in the natural level coming to

the Divine truth in the sensuous level, and successively becoming integrated into the Divine Human. The Lord on earth is becoming, successively, "Divine love in human form" (AC 4735). You feel this in reading the latter parts of the gospels, especially the gospel of John. You feel His love in the resurrection of Lazarus, in His giving the first Holy Supper, in His incredible steadfastness in His last temptations (see AC 9670:4).

Chapter Thirty-Seven

CELESTIAL LOVE AND CHARITY REUNITE

THE REUNION OF JOSEPH AND ISRAEL
GENESIS 46

+ Israel journeys toward Egypt, with all of his children and their families.

+ God assures him that He will make them a great nation in Egypt.

+ Israel and Joseph are reunited. They embrace and weep together.

Israel's belief that Joseph had been torn to pieces by a wild beast had haunted his life. To him, Joseph was dead. Within this conviction is one of the saddest realities of human life, the belief by adults that the Joseph within them, their earliest innocence, is lost, gone, and even more brutally, dead. **Israel believed this, and he had the evidence of the torn and bloody tunic.** The undamaged tunic or coat of many colors represents the wonderful variety of truths that infants believe with trust and innocence. These truths may be summarized in the infants' deep belief that the Lord made everything: that He is our Father Who tenderly cares for us every moment. In adult life, it seems that a wild beast destroys both this earliest innocence and its "childish" beliefs.

As time goes on in rebirth, Jacob takes on progressively higher representations. First he is truth in the natural level, then the goodness of truth there, and finally, as Israel, regenerate good there, or natural goodness that has been remade by truth. Now he has come to represent spiritual goodness from the natural level: the clear "charity" or active, everyday love of the neighbor that can come in old age to the faithful.

The ten brothers, who had also gradually reformed and been reborn, came back to Israel in Canaan and told him astonishing news:

" 'Joseph is still alive, and he has dominion in all the land of Egypt.' And Israel's heart failed, for he did not believe them. And they spoke to him all of Joseph's words which he had spoken to them; and he saw the carts which Joseph had sent to carry him, and the spirit of Jacob their father revived. And Israel said, 'Enough; Joseph my son is still alive. I will go and see him before I die' " (Gen. 45:26-28).

On rare occasions we find magical moments in life. Falling in love is one of them. Seeing truth as the Lord's truth is another. Discovering a love of others that is not selfish is another (this is Israel). But to find that Joseph has not died, that the innocence of infancy is still within us and alive — this is probably the highest spiritual experience in life. Very few people find this here on earth, but many, many people will find this after death. The Lord is within this realization, for He is the originator of our earliest remains. This rediscovered innocence blesses our love for our conjugial partner in ways inexpressible. The Lord says this state is one of "innocence, peace, tranquility, inmost friendship, full confidence, and a mutual desire of mind and heart to do the other every good" (CL 180).

Israel's journey to Egypt and being reunited with Joseph is charity, or active love of the neighbor, coming to celestial love and being conjoined with it. This changes the nature of the charity, for now it is being conjoined with the highest innocence and love in the human mind. It is conjoined with that gentle and trusting quality from the earliest times in our lives, a quality we had thought dead.

In Beersheba, as Israel started his journey down to reunite with Joseph,

"God spoke to Israel in visions of the night, and said, 'Jacob, Jacob.' And he said, 'Behold, here I am.' And He said, 'I am God, the God of your father; do not be afraid of going down to Egypt, for I will make you into a great nation there. I will also go down with you to Egypt, and I will certainly cause you to come up also, and Joseph will put his hand on your eyes' " (Gen. 46:2-4).

This was the God who had spoken to Jacob earlier in his life, at Bethel, when he was starting on his journey to Haran. Now again, God appeared to him. He reassured Jacob, now called Israel, and said concerning Joseph: "Joseph will put his hand on your eyes" (Gen. 46:4).

This statement, "Joseph will put his hand on your eyes," means that charity would have its inner eyes opened, opened by celestial love (AC 6008).

"And Israel traveled on and all that he had" (Gen. 46: 1). This traveling of Israel refers to the "beginning of the joining together" (AC 5996) of Israel and Joseph. This is a spiritual journey toward reunion, and is "a continuation of and further stage in the glorification of the Lord, Who in the highest sense is 'Israel' and 'Joseph,' whereas a continuation and further stage of a person's regeneration is meant in the internal sense" (*Ibid.*).

To bring the inmost of the human essence in the Lord (Joseph) to union with the spiritual goodness from His natural or outer level (Israel) is "a further stage in the glorification" (AC 5996). With Him, as with us in potential, spiritual progress is descending from inmosts to outmosts. Divine love is coming, bringing warmth and life to each successive level of the heart and thought.

When and if our "Israel" joins our "Joseph," it is like an angel putting his hand on our eyes. When his hand is removed, we see in a whole new way.

"And Joseph harnessed his chariot, and went up to meet Israel his father, to Goshen, and he was seen toward him [that is, Joseph presented himself to his father], and Joseph fell on his neck, and wept on his neck a long while. And Israel said to Joseph, 'Now let me die, after I have seen your face, that you are still alive' " (Gen. 46:29, 30).

Joseph's and Israel's embracing and weeping from love express this reunion of the inmost love with outer charity. **They were weeping and rejoicing because they had found each other. Joseph was not dead! And Israel had become a changed person.** These two, in their reunion, prophesy much for the spiritual future of this world. Some time in the future rebirth of humankind, inmost love from infancy and outer charity, or kindness to the neighbor, will reunite in many human hearts. Human charity from the Lord will have its eyes opened from inmost love. Peace and kindness will come to humankind in place of today's wars and cruelties. **Joseph will put his hand on Israel's eyes, and there will be a blessing.**

This is possible now, and will be in the future, because with the Lord Himself, in His glorification, Joseph and Israel are reunited. Jesus Christ is successively becoming the Divine good, even as with Benjamin, and earlier with Isaac, He had become Divine truth. "His Human was made Divine truth when He was in the world, thus such as is in heaven. But afterwards it was successively made Divine Good of Divine Love by union with the Father" (Ath. Cr. 156).

This reunion of Joseph and Israel is another of the key stages in the Lord's process of becoming Divine goodness on this earth. This process was not completed until the end of His temptation on the cross, when "He made His human Divine Good" (AC 9670:4). The specific words here are: "When He departed out of the world, He made His Human Divine good" (*Ibid.*). Still, Israel's and Joseph's reunion is a great step in this process.

Two primary truths are revealed here. One, as we have seen, concerns the reunion of inmost innocence and charity or love of the neighbor. The other focuses on "the joining together of the Church's truths and its factual knowledges" (AC 6047:2). Examples of these "factual knowledges" are the beauty of creation, the facts of science, the history of civilization, and the origin of the human species. This introduction of spiritual truths into the facts that we know is represented by Jacob's taking his whole family down to the land of Egypt (which represents worldly knowledge) to meet Joseph. The name "Jacob" is used in this case, not Israel. "The reason why the name 'Jacob' and not Israel is used is that natural truth and all that accompanied it must be introduced into the facts known to the Church, meant by Jacob's going down into Egypt together with his sons" (AC 6001).

Jacob represents natural-level truth here, but behind this is the powerful inflowing of Divine rational truth within the Lord. This is what is meant by the verse: **"And God said, 'I am the God of your father' "** (Gen. 46:3). This "father" is Isaac, the Divine rational. The following phrase: **"Do not be afraid of going down to Egypt"** (Gen. 46:3) "means that natural truth and all that accompanies it *must* be introduced into the facts known to the Church" (AC 6004, emphasis added). This word "must" is used firmly, and means that such introduction of spiritual truths into worldly facts is necessary if we would find the Lord and be reborn. When truths are so introduced, then "when some fact comes to mind, the truths that have been gathered into it may be recollected at the same time" (AC 6004:3).

"It is an essential of Divine order that interior things should be gathered into exterior ones, so that finally everything prior should be gathered into what is last and lowest and coexist with it. This is what happens in the entire creation. If this were not so, no one could be fully regenerated" (AC 6004:4).

Truths gathered into facts, and ordering them, enable what is interior within our hearts to become one with what is outmost — the things of our senses. This brings heaven to earth.

". . .Knowledge dwells in virtually the same inferior light as a person's physical sight. This inferior light is such that unless it is brightened from within by the light received from truths, it leads to falsities, especially those that are produced by the illusions of the senses" (*Ibid.*).

This is a call to become aware that behind all the beauty of creation, the facts of science, the history of civilization, the origin of the human species, is the hand of the Divine Creator. When inner loves, truths, and data are ordered from above, we are open to the song of David:

"O Lord, our Lord, how excellent is Your name in all the earth, You Who set Your glory above the heavens. . . .When I consider Your heavens, the work of Your fingers, the moon and stars which You have ordained, what is man that You are mindful of him, and the Son of Man that You visit Him?" (Psalm 8:1,3-4)

All this is based on a fundamental premise that innocence (a willingness to be led by the Lord) can see what conceit refuses to see. Innocence sees that there is a Lord, in His Divine Human, Who created each of us, Who loves us, and Who made all of creation in order to lead us in freedom to heaven.

It is the Joseph in us that sees. **This Joseph welcomes Jacob and all his children and belongings into Egypt.** He welcomes truths and goods and innocence into the Egypt of sensual and scientific knowledge. For the senses and sciences will gradually become truly alive for us, brightened by the Lord's charity and light. But it will still take some time. **There is still a famine in the land of Egypt that must be faced and overcome.** But the Lord is coming to us, even to our senses.

Chapter Thirty-Eight

REBIRTH OF THE SENSUOUS

DEALING WITH THE FAMINE
GENESIS 47

+ Joseph tells Pharaoh of his family's arrival.

+ They settle in the land of Goshen, in Egypt.

+ The famine remains very severe. When people run out of money to buy grain from Joseph, he offers to trade them the grain for livestock.

+ When the livestock runs out, Joseph accepts land from the people in exchange for food. The land would now belong to Pharaoh. The people would still work the land, but give one fifth of their future crops to Pharaoh.

Joseph told Pharaoh his good news: Joseph's father and brothers had come with all their possessions to settle in the land of Egypt. Pharaoh welcomed this from his heart, for Joseph had been the savior of Egypt during the famine. Now Pharaoh could show kindness in return.

" 'The land of Egypt is before you; in the best of the land cause your father and your brothers to dwell; let them dwell in the land of Goshen. . . .' And Joseph caused Jacob his father to

come, and placed him before Pharaoh; and Jacob blessed
Pharaoh. . . .And Joseph sustained his father and his brothers,
and all his father's household with bread" (Gen. 47:6,7,12).

Pharaoh represents knowledge in the lower level of our mind.
As this lower level is ordered by inmost innocence, it welcomes
charity (Israel) with deepest respect, and looks to the truths in the
natural (the sons of Jacob) to be shepherds in the land. Such shepherds represent true ideas that lead to a good life and which use the
land of Pharaoh (knowledges) wisely (see AC 6059, 6060).

This welcoming of Joseph, Jacob, and Jacob's sons by Pharaoh
indicates (representatively) a mind receptive of the Lord, a looking
in trust to the Lord in His Divine Human. When Joseph rules and
sustains his father and brothers, things are favorable in human states.
Things are favorable for the over-all rebirth of the human mind.
With our cooperation and consent, the rational level, together with
the natural, has already been reborn from the Lord's operations. The
very sensuous, the lowest level, has begun to be truly ordered.

But one tends to forget, when seeing the affirmative progress,
that **"There was no bread in all the land, for the famine was
extremely serious; and the land of Egypt and the land of
Canaan languished from the presence of the famine" (Gen.
47:13).** Famine is a lack of goodness: here, in Egypt, a lack of
goodness in the sensuous level. When there is famine on this lowest level, there is also a famine in the higher level of the mind, in
Canaan. This has its counterpart in the New Testament in the
absence of good with many of the Pharisees.

Despite all the good things that have happened to us, we still
feel desolation within. Something vital is missing. Our lowest level
of thinking and feeling is out of kilter, desperately hungry for good.
We are uneasy, searching for the Lord in things of the sensuous
level. Why are our senses not alive to inner beauty and love? Why
are our knowledges, though ordered from above, still not sparkling,
seemingly devoid of real life?

Something powerful and subtle is standing in the way. This is hereditary evil, still hidden within our sensuous level. It is the strong sense that outer truths and the good we feel outwardly are *ours*, and certainly our bodies are *ours* and not the Lord's. Where there is an insistence of self-life, that all things are from self, the Lord cannot enter. No matter how regenerate our rational or higher natural level may be, if the lower level is still a rebel, it affects states within. There is a famine. Once again, it is another, and stronger, nighttime of the senses.

When we read: **"The famine was extremely serious" (Gen. 47:13),** it "means desolation" (AC 6110). This is the despair that comes when good seems to be gone in our outer life.

"And Joseph gathered all the silver found in the land of Egypt and in the land of Canaan, for the corn which they were buying; and Joseph caused the silver to come to Pharaoh's house" (Gen. 47:14). When we feel desolation and despair, the Lord comes with aid and healing. He gives an inner food that sustains and gives life to our hungry states. He gives us corn, or wheat. But in return for this good, this "daily bread," we give Him our silver. We do this willingly.

Silver here corresponds to "knowledge that held truth in it" (AC 6112). In our sensuous level, and our understanding there, we give up possession of such knowledge that holds truth. That is, we stop insisting inwardly that these are ours. Rather, we see these facts as part of a general whole, part of the Lord's genuine pattern of creation. We now realize that all the ideas we take pride in knowing come from associate good spirits, and ultimately from the Lord. Our every thought comes from Him. We must come to <u>want</u> to ascribe these facts, and the truths within them, to the Lord Himself. "The most general and all-embracing whole, the source from which everything is held in place is the Lord Himself; and what holds everything in place is Divine Truth going forth from Him" (AC 6115:3).

With Jesus Christ on earth, this is a far-advanced stage of glorification. He now is being further glorified even as to His sensuous level. This is a step-by-step glorification, and continues now with direct focus on the sensuous level inherited through Mary that ascribes facts and their truths to itself. This is being changed. Jesus is rejecting this falsity, cleansing it out of His sensuous. He experiences and lives this state of glorification.

"And when the silver was used up in the land of Egypt and in the land of Canaan, all Egypt came to Joseph, saying, 'Give us bread; and why should we die nearby you because the silver is lacking?' And Joseph said, 'Give your livestock, and I will give you [bread] in exchange for your livestock, if the silver is lacking.' And they caused their livestock to come to Joseph, and Joseph gave them bread in exchange for horses, and for livestock of the flock, and for livestock of the herd, and for asses; and he provided them with bread in exchange for all their livestock that year" (Gen. 47:15-17).

Bread for livestock! The famine was eased; food was purchased. The desolation (within) eased off when the Egyptians gave up their farm animals. What do the livestock mean in our rebirth and the Lord's glorification? The plea for bread is "a plea for the sustainment of spiritual life" (AC 6118). When the silver is gone, when knowledges with their truths are yielded up, there comes in time "a state of desolation" — "truth seems to have fled" (AC 6122). It hasn't really fled, for "all truth and good that the Lord ever grants a person, spirit, or angel remains. None is ever taken away from them, but in a state of desolation they become so obscured by the person's selfhood that they cannot be seen" (*Ibid.*).

Here is the cause of obscurity, of famine: "the person's selfhood" cuts off heavenly influx. Knowledges with their truths (silver) have been totally ascribed to the Lord. But now something even more meaningful, loves with their truth in the sensuous level seem gone (AC 6123). Loves in the natural or sensuous level that spring from truths there — these have sustained us and fed us. But as the famine continues, even these loves with their truths must be transferred to the Lord. The livestock, which represent our outer sensual loves, must be given to Joseph in return for bread. In extreme desolation, we realize that even the loves we have felt in our outer life have not been ours actually. We find at the end of temptation a new realization. These outer loves are actually also the Lord's! When we can make this ascription with honesty and insight, the Lord does a wonderful thing. He inflows with bread from heaven. He sustains us.

Again, this is a new step forward in the rebirth of the sensuous. Seeing this ends the famine we have known through many states. Truth and knowledges we have honestly given to the Lord. Now love, too, we ascribe to Him, love in all its various forms in our outer mind. These loves are defined by the *delights* they give: they include all good sensuous delights. These would be delights in the beauty of nature with its seasons, delights in human artistic expressions, delights in nourishing food and drink, delights of conjugial love in ultimates. These various forms of delight and their loves are represented by the variety of livestock handed over to Joseph. This new insight, this new ascription from the heart, feeds us with heavenly food.

"**And that year ended, and they came to Joseph in the second year, and said to him, 'We will not hide from [my] lord, that since the silver has been used up and the livestock of the beasts has passed to [my] lord, nothing is left before [my] lord apart from our bodies and our ground. Why should we die before your eyes, both we and our ground? Buy us and our ground for bread, and we will live, and our ground, as Pharaoh's slaves; and give us seed so that we may live and not die, and the ground may not become a waste'**" (Gen. 47:18,19).

"**Nothing is left before [my] lord apart from our bodies and our ground.**" This is the giving up of the belief of our proprium (our feeling of selfhood) that our outmost life, our bodies and their sensations *are ours*. Outermost life and sensations come through receptacles on the sensuous level: the five senses and the strong appearance of self-life there. Once before there was a challenge and temptations on this level in a general way. We find this in the story of the butler and baker and their dreams. But now these lowest receptacles of life meet severe temptations. This is the final refusal from our proprium to ascribe physical life and its sensations to the Lord. The contemporary demand by some to retain complete control of their bodies, with the right to commit suicide, or the right to abort fetuses in *all* cases, expresses this lowest physical thinking. This is the last outpost of evil's self-love. This is also the case if we abuse our bodies with harmful substances, believing that our bodies are ours to do with as we feel. If we wish to confirm this appearance, then we limit ourselves in a stark way, for there is a stage beyond this that finally invites the Lord to enter our hearts fully.

We cannot pass through this blockade, this temptation, without feeling terrible desolation. Old people sometimes show this, especially when the spiritual temptation involved is also combined with physical suffering or handicaps. Again, the Lord does not permit this in order to punish us. Rather, it enables us to find Him as we never have before. **The people of Egypt gave up their bodies, their labor, to Joseph. And they gave up their ground to him and Pharaoh. In return, Joseph and Pharaoh gave back four-fifths of all the harvests with one-fifth coming to Pharaoh. This was true of all except the priests.**

What is happening here? At first we sense terrible depression and desolation. Then the realization gradually dawns: our bodies are only receptacles, receptacles of delights and sensations. But their *life* really is the Lord's life in us. We then can actually rise above our bodies and not let them be the origin of anxiety. We perceive too that the spiritual body is within our natural one and that we will enter into this spiritual body with its health and youth upon leaving this world.

The body in true order is a receptacle of life and of good from the Lord (AC 6135).

"I [Swedenborg] have been able to see quite clearly from the angels that 'body' in the genuine sense is the good of love. When they [the angels] are present, love floods out of their entire bodies. Also their bodies have a dazzling appearance full of light shining from them; for the good of love is like a flame sending out from itself light, which is the truth of faith derived from that good.

"If this therefore is what the angels of heaven are like, what of the Lord Himself? He is the source of every spark of love among the angels, and His Divine Love is seen as the Sun. . . .The Lord's Divine Human is what appears in that way and is the Source of all those things. From this one may now see what is meant by the Lord's body – Divine Love, the same as is meant by His flesh. . . .Also, the Lord's very body – having been glorified, that is made Divine – is nothing else than such Love. . . .Nothing else is meant by 'body' in the Holy Supper than the Lord's Divine Love toward the entire human race" (AC 6135:3,4).

The desolation of the Egyptians (and of the Egyptians in us) leads them *not* to annihilation, but instead to a reception of Divine Love that is transforming. This is pictured in the Holy Supper, inaugurated by the Lord on the Thursday of Easter week. The bread received by His disciples is His Divine love, and the wine is His wisdom. This indicates what happens to the Lord Jesus Christ at the culmination of His glorification. He becomes the "bread of life." His Body becomes Divine: Divine Love itself.

The temptations and desolation represented by giving up the silver, cattle, bodies and ground are nearly the final temptations of human regeneration. And with the Lord too, these are almost the last temptations. They are certainly near if not identical with the temptations in the garden of Gethsemane, when "His sweat became like great drops of blood falling down to the ground" (Luke 22:44).

In return for offering up their bodies and ground, the Egyptians would be given "seed" for crops, which represents "an influx. . .of the good of charity and the truth of faith" (AC 6139). They asked for this seed "so that we may live and not die," which means "spiritual life received. . .and the fear of damnation no longer" (AC 6140). This seed they would plant in the earth (goodness in the sensuous level), awaiting rain from heaven or irrigation from the Nile. "The fear of damnation no longer" – these are the sweetest words, and they speak to a fear of old people and of many others.

Of Joseph's final steps to feed the Egyptians through the years of famine, it is said that "only the ground of the priests he did not buy, for the priests had a fixed portion from Pharaoh and ate their fixed portion which Pharaoh had given them; therefore they did not sell their ground" (Gen. 47:22). The "ground of the priests" here refers to the capacities or talents to receive good and truth from the Lord.

"A person's capacities to receive truth and good come directly from the Lord; he obtains them without any help at all from himself. A person's capacity to receive goodness and truth is maintained in him unceasingly. . . .But a person does not receive them if he turns to evil. The capacity to receive does, it is true, remain, but its access to thought and sensitivity is blocked, on account of which his capacity to see what is true and have a sensitive awareness of what is good perishes" (AC 6148:2).

Our abilities, our talents, and our receptions of loves and insights — these come from the Lord. He gives them to us as talents without any help from ourselves. Sometimes we forget this and become elated over our own abilities and creativity. What seems to happen then, very often, is that our wells dry up! We easily lose visions and new insights when we get conceited. The painting will not come, or the writing encounters a mental block. Things seem to go wrong with our creative endeavors. I think this happens in order to lead us to a truth: our talents are gifts from the Lord. Gifts are given and are not bartered for. The greatest artists seem to be aware of this, as when a composer like Handel says that a work like "The Messiah" comes from the Lord.

Chapter Thirty-Nine

A New Understanding and Will in the Sensuous

Blessings of Ephraim and Manasseh
Genesis 48

+ Israel (Jacob) becomes sick, and is near death.

+ Joseph brings his two sons to his father so that they may receive his blessing.

+ Joseph puts his older son, Manasseh, at Israel's right hand to receive the greater blessing.

+ Israel, however, crosses his arms and puts his right hand on the head of Ephraim, the younger son, and his left hand on the head of Manasseh.

+ This displeases Joseph, but Israel says it must be so.

Israel was now an old man, and his eyes were dim so that he could not see clearly. Realizing that his father was about to die, Joseph brought his two sons to Israel hoping for his blessing. Israel was told: "Behold, your son Joseph has come to you. And Israel strengthened himself, and sat on the bed" (Gen. 48:2). He reminisced then about outstanding events in his lifetime, things that had touched his heart. He spoke of God's appearing to him in Luz (or Bethel), with that vision of the ladder ascending to

heaven, and of God's blessing him then.

Israel spoke warmly to Joseph of his sons: "And now your two sons. . .they are mine, Ephraim and Manasseh. As Reuben and Simeon they shall be mine" (Gen. 48:5). Jacob represents the truth in Jesus' natural-level mind. Into this level have come truth and goodness (Ephraim and Manasseh) from a deeper source (Joseph)(see AC 6234-6238). This brings great joy to Jesus, as Joseph's sons bring great joy to Jacob.

He also spoke of another memory which still moved him deeply: "And as for me, when I was coming from Paddan, Rachel died on me in the land of Canaan on the road when there was still a stretch of land to go to Ephrath; and I buried her there on the road to Ephrath (that is, Bethlehem)" (Gen. 48:7). Bethlehem, where the Lord was later to be born! A sphere of the Lord touches this verse; for Israel represents the Divine good in the Lord, and Rachel, Israel's beloved wife, is the interior love of truth. Bethlehem, where Jesus was later to be born, is the spiritual of the celestial: truth seen clearly from love, even the Lord's Divine truth seen clearly from Divine Good.

Israel rejoiced at the chance to bless Ephraim and Manasseh, Joseph's two sons born in Egypt. He said to Joseph: "I did not think to see your face, and behold, God has caused me to see your seed also" (Gen. 48:11). The blessings that follow have an interesting correspondence. **Joseph presented Manasseh to Israel's right hand and Ephraim to Israel's left hand.** In ancient biblical times, the right hand gave the priority and higher blessing.

But Israel did a strange thing. He did this even though he could not see well, being led to an enactment that came directly from God. "Israel put out his right hand and placed it on Ephraim's head, who was the younger, and his left hand on Manasseh's head; crosswise he put out his hands. . . ." (Gen. 48:14). In so blessing them, he said: "May God bless the boys, and in them will my name be called, and the name of my fathers

Abraham and Isaac; and may they increase into a multitude in the midst of the earth" (Gen. 48:16).

Joseph tried to correct Israel's error in his placing his right hand on Ephraim's head and his left on Manasseh's, the first-born. "Joseph saw that his father placed his right hand on Ephraim's head, and it was wrong in his eyes" (Gen. 48:17). But Israel refused to make a change. He said: "I know, my son, I know; he [Manasseh] too will be a people, and he too will be great; but truly, his younger brother will become greater than he, and his seed will be the fullness of nations" (Gen. 48:19).

The chapter concludes: "And Israel said to Joseph, 'Behold, I am dying; and God will be with you, and will bring you back to the land of your fathers. And I give you one portion above your brothers, which I took out of the hand of the Amorite with my sword and my bow' " (Gen. 48:21,22).

The deeper meaning within this chapter treats of the role of Ephraim and Manasseh in the glorification of the Lord's sensuous level, and of the rebirth of our sensuous level. Within us, Manasseh represents the *new will* in the natural, and Ephraim the *new understanding* in the natural (AC 6222; cf. AC 6234, 6236). The natural includes a number of levels ranging from the rational to the sensuous, and even to the body in the widest definition. The rational has already been reborn, as has the higher level of the natural. We see this in the stories of Isaac and Jacob, renamed Israel. That Joseph and his life are tied to the rebirth of the sensuous is quite evident in the *Arcana* treatment of the dreams of the butler and the baker.

This rebirth comes in the final stages of regeneration, and in these stages nature opens up as the Lord's heaven on earth. It sings and speaks from within of heavenly life. Nature becomes again, as it was with the Most Ancient peoples, a medium of contact with the angels (AC 1802-6).

This is possible because the Lord reaches this stage of the glorification: His Sensuous is made Divine. He establishes the path of

Ephraim (a new understanding) as being first in His sensuous, and then Manasseh (a new will).

It is interesting that as Israel blessed his grandsons, Ephraim, the younger came first and Manasseh second. Truth or understanding (Ephraim) leads the way to the rebirth of goodness on the sensuous level, just as truth takes first leadership on the higher levels of the mind. Earlier in Biblical and spiritual history, Jacob came before Esau. Truth coming into our understanding must happen first in rebirth. Later in Genesis (Genesis 38), there are Perez and Zerah, born of Tamar and Judah. Perez symbolizes the first truth to regenerate the sensuous, and Zerah the first good that follows (see Chapter 27, *The Path*). If we try to put our will first, prior to applying the discipline of truth, we inevitably go astray, for our will at each level is flawed until truth seemingly leads the way and establishes genuine order. The word "seemingly" (AC 6217) is used because behind any self-discipline obtained by means of revealed truth is the motivating factor in our will of earliest remains: remains of goodness! Though we seem to compel ourselves sometimes to live according to true principles "against our will," it is really the hidden remains of goodness in our will which motivate us to do so!

Our sensuous level is the nest or home of hereditary evil tendencies. We need only look at the disorders on the sensuous level in the world, and look into our own hearts and motivations, to see that the senses are easily prone to evil. "The flesh is weak" (Matt. 26:41).

The Lord, however, leads us past the Ephraim stage of self-compulsion, even to the Manasseh state: to the birth of a new will in the sensuous itself, which allows the Lord to flow with His warmth into our outer earth, to our senses. This means that the body stops ruling us. Sensual delights become subordinate; heavenly loves are uppermost. Charity and love lead instead of bodily lusts and anxieties. It was Joseph who saw a truth when it came to the genuine relationship of Manasseh and Ephraim. **It was "wrong in**

his eyes" (Gen. 48: 17) that Israel gave priority of blessing to Ephraim.

The *Arcana* explains that the phrase "it was wrong in his eyes" means "displeasure."

"The reason why Joseph was displeased was that he represents the internal celestial, which is above the spiritual good that 'Israel' represents. What is higher can discern the nature of anything done in what is lower, and so can also discern whether or not any thought there is the truth. . . .What is higher can see whatever exists in lower parts, because it does so in the light of heaven. . . .The internal celestial, which is 'Joseph,' could see that spiritual good from the natural, which is 'Israel,' was making a mistake" (AC 6288).

In the long run, good always has priority over truth. The internal celestial (Joseph) sees this clearly. But in the shorter run, in the process of rebirth, truth seemingly takes priority over goodness for a time. Israel was right in the short run; Joseph was right eternally (AC 6240)!

"And Israel said to Joseph, 'Behold I am dying; and God will be with you, and will bring you back to the land of your fathers' " (Gen. 48:21). "Dying" means "awaking to life" (AC 6302), and with Israel this means "new life" (*Ibid.*). The Divine good in the Lord's natural level represented by Israel is now being glorified. This is a truly tremendous step in those successive stages by which the Lord became Divine good (Ath. Cr. 156, AC 2649). Gone would be a major blockage from the Lord's finite maternal heredity, which had connected impurity with sensuous delight. Through His process, Jesus rediscovers and re-establishes the Divine in the human sensuous level. He can feel more fully than ever the Divine goodness and truth that exist there. There are only the final steps to be taken: the complete glorification of the sensuous level and the body.

Chapter Forty

A REVIEW OF THE GLORIFICATION

ISRAEL'S FINAL BLESSINGS
GENESIS 49

+ Israel gives final blessings or curses to his sons.

+ He instructs them to bury him with his ancestors, and then he dies.

The final two chapters of Genesis bring the history of Israel and then of Joseph to fulfilling ends. Israel, an old man, called his twelve sons to him, and by Divine leadership gave blessings or curses to each son. In these blessings we find some of the most touching poetry of the Word. The last verse of Genesis 49 reads: "And Jacob finished commanding his sons, and he gathered up his feet toward the bed, and expired, and was gathered to his peoples" (v. 33).

"And was gathered to his peoples." In this is a truth that speaks of death as the angels see it. It is not the end. It is rather the true beginning, the fulfillment of the purpose of life on earth. Death then, in the spiritual sense, means new life. In this there is the heartbeat of hope rather than any lasting tragedy. Israel was "gathered to his peoples" in the spiritual world. By this great step in Israel's life is meant the Lord's coming into Divine good in His natural as a

240

whole. This Divine good is His intense, compassionate love for each human being ever born.

When did He become Divine good or love on this natural plane? In the Old Testament, it was when Israel finished his blessings and then died. In the New Testament, it was at the conclusion of the temptation in the Garden of Gethsemane. He then "rose up from prayer, and came to His disciples" (Luke 22:45). To "rise up" is to be elevated into a new state, and with Jesus here, into Divine good or love itself on the natural plane. This coming into Divine good helps Him to face the betrayal, trials, persecution, and crucifixion that are to come. He faces these with Divine love, not with defeating despair. But the finite human level was still present in His senses and body. The sensuous level is not yet the Divine Good (Ath. Cr. 156).

Both Israel and Joseph came into peace and fulfillment before their deaths. Each came into a golden state. The New Testament gives much of the shock and temptations of the Lord's last days on earth, but words of hope are there as well. However, it is in the Old Testament, in the story of the final days of Israel and Joseph, that the Lord's love and hopes in these last few days are more fully revealed.

"And Jacob called his sons, and said, 'Gather together, and I will tell you what will happen to you at the end of days. Assemble and hear, O sons of Jacob, and hear Israel your father' " (Genesis 49:1,2).

What follows are both curses and blessings of the sons. Certain ones are cursed, and certain ones are blessed. The twelve sons with us represent major qualities that comprise the human mind: those goods and truths, or their opposites, that make up a human being. Why, at the end of His life on this earth, did the Lord make this summation of qualities composing the human mind? It reminds me of the discovery that, when near death and resurrection, a person experiences a quick review of his entire history,

241

his entire lifetime on earth. Did the Lord experience such a review now of His entire glorification?

Israel's blessings and curses seem to be a summation of the glorification itself: a brief, clear overview of the Divine process. First, in the curses of Reuben, Simeon, and Levi, it exposes qualities in the finite human heredity through Mary. Then comes a presentation of the human Divine, those qualities of the celestial kingdom that the Lord assumed when "He bowed the heavens. . .and came down" (Psalm 18:9). Judah represents this human Divine.

Then follow Zebulun, Issachar, Dan, Gad, Asher, and Naphtali. The "blessings" contain, in some cases, an unveiling of the negative or finite human hereditary qualities, and then the Divine qualities, which become present after temptation and glorification. They seem to be an outline of the glorifying of the Human, Jesus, that Jehovah assumed on earth. Following this is a soaring, uplifting song which is in the blessing upon Joseph. This seems in the celestial sense to be a portrayal of the Divine Human glorified. It shows Joseph in his glory, even as the transfiguration showed the Lord in His glory. Benjamin follows last, as the Divine brother of Joseph.

Three of these sons of Israel now especially deserve study and reflection. They signify highest qualities of the Lord Jesus Christ and their effects with us, the Lord's children.

Of Judah, Israel said:

"Judah are you, your brothers will praise you; your hand will be on the neck of your enemies. Your father's sons will bow down to you. A lion's cub is Judah; from the plunder you have gone up, my son. He crouched, he lay down like a lion, and like an old lion; who will rouse him? The scepter will not be removed from Judah, nor the lawgiver from between his feet, until Shiloh comes; and to him will be the obedience of the peoples. He binds his young ass to the vine, and the foal of his she-ass to the outstanding vine; he washes his clothing in wine, and

his garment in the blood of grapes. His eyes are red from wine, and his teeth white from milk" (Gen. 49:11).

Judah is the celestial church (AC 6363), that is, all those who live from an innocent love of the Lord. This church is "superior to all the rest" (AC 6364). The hells flee from the celestial; its innocence puts terror into evil. In this innocence is an "innate strength" (AC 6367), which is depicted as a "lion's cub." After being called a lion's cub, Judah is likened to a young lion and an old lion. This is the power of the celestial, which "is safe when among all those in the hells" (AC 6370).

The Most Ancient Church on this earth, and the celestial heaven that is made up of people from this church, manifested humankind as the Lord intended. Its innocence, trust, and wisdom were those of wise children: **"The scepter will not be removed from Judah, nor a lawgiver from between his feet, until Shiloh comes" (Gen. 49:10).** Before the Lord became incarnate, He inflowed into the good people on this earth through the celestial kingdom, the celestial angels. When He appeared to Old Testament leaders and prophets, He appeared through a celestial angel. The Lord's power on earth then rested with these angels: through them He touched the hearts of people upon earth. This presence of Jehovah was called the human Divine (AC 2814). Judah represented these celestial angels, and this prophecy said that the scepter would not depart from Judah until Shiloh comes.

What the Lord lacked before His incarnation was a body visible to our minds and hearts. He did not have what is called the Divine natural (see TCR 109). He could not inflow *directly* into human minds on earth; He needed to go through Judah, the celestial kingdom. This was effective until humankind experienced the fall into evil. As soon as the fall took place, the Lord prophesied in Genesis 3:15 that He would be born on earth: "And I will put enmity between you [the serpent] and the woman, and between your seed and her Seed. He shall bruise your head, and you shall bruise

His heel." This "He" is the Lord Jesus Christ, to be born of the virgin Mary.

After the fall of humankind, human beings fell more and more deeply into evil, and the celestial kingdom (Judah) proved weaker and weaker in reaching down to affect and reform human hearts. Judah did reign, the "scepter" did not depart from Judah, nor a "lawgiver from between his feet," until Shiloh came. The "lawgiver from between his feet" means truths through the celestial angels in lower things (AC 6372). But this truth, too, was becoming less and less effective (see AC 6373). It could not reach down into the lower, fallen natural and sensual levels in which people were living.

Then "Shiloh" came! The Lord Jesus Christ was born on earth, an infant babe in Bethlehem of Judea. The coming of Shiloh means "the Lord's coming, and the peaceful tranquility at that time. This is clear from the meaning of 'Shiloh' as the Lord, Who is called Shiloh because He brought peace to all things and gave them tranquility; for in the original language Shiloh is derived from a word meaning tranquil" (AC 6373).

After Israel's prophecy concerning Judah, six other sons received their "blessings." Then follows the blessing upon Joseph. Joseph represents the "Shiloh" who was to come, the "Shiloh" Who would restore Divine truth and the power of the Lord to free and touch human hearts.

Of Joseph, Israel said:

"The son of a fertile one is Joseph, the son of a fertile one beside a spring. . . .He will sit in the strength of his bow, and the arms of his hands are made strong by the hands of the powerful Jacob — from there is the shepherd, the stone of Israel. By the God of your father, Who will help you, and together with Shaddai, Who will bless you with the blessings of heaven from above, the blessings of the deep lying beneath, the blessings of the breasts and of the womb. The blessings of your father will prevail over the blessings of my ancestors, even as far as the

desire of the everlasting hills. They will be on the head of Joseph, and on the crown of the head of the Nazarite among his brothers" (Gen. 49:22-26, selections).

Each phrase in Israel's blessing of Joseph speaks of potentials for each one of us. "Since 'Joseph' is the fruitfulness of good and the multiplication of truth, he is called (in Israel's blessing) 'the son of a fertile one' " (AC 6417). That Joseph "will sit in the strength of his bow" (Gen. 49:24) and that his arms "are made strong by the hands of the powerful Jacob" (*Ibid.*) describe the power that can be gained from revealed truth that is truly present in "doctrine," or religious principles (AC 6423). Also the fact that power will inflow through this truth "from the almighty power of the Lord's Divine Human" (AC 6425, see 6424).

Joseph's blessing speaks of the "shepherd, the stone of Israel" (Gen. 49:24). Inmostly, this Shepherd surely is the Lord, for a shepherd spiritually is "one who leads to the good of charity by means of the truth of faith" (AC 6426). The 23rd Psalm tells of reality: "The Lord is my Shepherd." And the "stone of Israel" here "is used in the highest sense to mean the Lord" (AC 6426:3). This "stone which the builders rejected has become the head of the corner" (Psalm 118:22).

In further speaking of Joseph in his blessing, Israel prophesied: "By the God of your father, Who will help you, and together with Shaddai, Who will bless you with the blessings of heaven from above, the blessings of the deep lying beneath, the blessings of the breasts and of the womb" (Gen. 49:25). The "God of your father" is "the God of the Ancient Church" (AC 6428). "God Shaddai" means "the Lord, the bringer of benefits after temptations" (AC 6429).

From the Lord a regenerating person will receive **"blessings of heaven from above" (Gen. 49:25).** These "mean blessings with goodness and truth from a source within" (AC 6430). This tells of love and faith touching us tenderly from within, changing our nature. Also given are **"blessings of the deep lying beneath"** **(Gen. 49:25)**, which tell of factual knowledges marvelously ordered by Divine truth. When revealed truth orders our perceptions of science and nature, it transforms them into real blessings. Outer creation becomes a theater representative of the Lord and of His heaven, as it was in earliest times (AC 1802-6).

The **"blessings of the breasts"** mean special affections of "goodness and truth" (AC 6432), which is the gentleness of conjugial love, received from the Lord. The breasts "mean those affections, because the breasts communicate with the generative organs, and for that reason belong to the province of conjugial love. . . .In addition they derive that meaning from the fact that the breasts are what feed infants, and so mean, through the affection that goes with breast-feeding, conjugial love when joined to the love of offspring" (*Ibid.*). The final words of this verse speak of the Lord giving blessings **"of the womb."** This means inmost love and faith "joined together" (AC 6433). "This is clear from the meaning of 'the womb' as the inmost center of conjugial love" (*Ibid.*). The Lord's pearl of great price is the restoration of conjugial love, the love between one man and one woman, which comes in innocence from the Lord.

Israel then promises: **"The blessings of your father will prevail over the blessings of my ancestors, even as far as the desire of the everlasting hills" (Gen. 49:26).** To people on earth now this offers special promise. For blessings that go as far "as the desire of the everlasting hills" mean "as far as celestial mutual love" (AC 6435), that is, a more deep and genuine love of the neighbor that flows out from an innocent love of the Lord. The hope for the Church on earth is for it to progress, under the Lord's leadership, to a return to a golden age, but now a new golden age of celestial love (see AC 6435:1,3).

Following the blessing of Joseph, we read of Benjamin:

"Benjamin is a wolf; he will seize in the morning, he will

devour the spoil, and at evening he will divide the plunder"
(Gen. 49:27). How strange! Why, after the beautiful blessing upon
Joseph, is Benjamin cursed? Why do the blessings end by seeming
to curse the youngest son?

But this is a case where affirmative, not negative, representatives rule. This is *not* a curse; it is a blessing! Benjamin is truth of
celestial good (AC 6440). He is, as we have seen before, new truth,
and the only truth of the church (see AC 6440). He is also defined
as "the spiritual of the celestial" (AC 9592), living truth from the
highest level open to us. That here he is called a wolf, "means an
eagerness to rescue and deliver the good. . . .It is evident [from literal passages in the Word] that 'a wolf' means those who seize, but
here one who rescues from hell those who have been seized" (AC
6441). This passage points out that a lion is also a rapacious animal,
"but in the good sense 'lion' means truth when empowered by
good. (The Lord Himself is likened to a lion.) Something similar
applies also to other ravenous creatures, such as leopards or eagles"
(*Ibid.*).

That Benjamin " 'will seize in the morning, he will devour the
spoil' means that the deliverance takes place when the Lord is present" (AC 6442). " 'And in the evening he will divide the plunder'
means their possession in the Lord's kingdom" (AC 6443).
Benjamin here represents a powerful and liberating quality in the
Lord's Divine Human glorified: this is His "eagerness to rescue and
deliver the good" (AC 6441). He will rescue them from evil states
as they respond in freedom to His new truth [Benjamin], and He
will lift them into the Lord's kingdom. When this happens, those
rescued will be "at first in obscurity" (AC 6443), but eventually
they will come into clear light (*Ibid.*). In an affirmative passage, it
is said: "There is little Benjamin, their leader..." (Psalm 68:27).

"All these are the twelve tribes of Israel, and this is what
their father spoke to them, and he blessed them, each according
to his blessing he blessed them. And Israel commanded them

and said to them, 'I am being gathered to my people; bury me with my fathers, at the cave, which is in the field of Ephron the Hittite, in the cave which is in the field of Machpelah, which faces Mamre in the land of Canaan, which Abraham bought. . . .There they buried Abraham and Sarah his wife; there they buried Isaac and Rebekah his wife; and there I buried Leah. . . .' And Jacob finished commanding his sons, and he gathered up his feet toward the bed, and expired, and was gathered to his people" (Gen. 49:28-33, selections).

Abraham is the Lord's celestial from childhood, which is glorified; Isaac is His rational, which is glorified; Jacob is His natural, which also is glorified.

The cave of Machpelah then, to the angels and the Lord, is a place of *life*, of wondrous entrance into glory. That Jacob now died, and was "gathered to his people" is the next-to-last stage of the glorification.

Joseph still lives in the nearly glorified Jesus Christ. Joseph is still the celestial of the spiritual in His human essence not yet glorified. This alone, along with His outer senses and body, is still finite. The last chapter of Genesis tells of this final glorification. It gives a different aspect to the Easter story itself.

Chapter Forty-One

ANGUISH, RECONCILIATION, GLORIFICATION

THE FINAL YEARS OF JOSEPH
GENESIS 50

> ✦ There is a great ceremony honoring the embalming and burial of Israel, with mourning by Joseph and his family, and also by the Egyptians.

> ✦ Joseph tenderly assures his brothers that he has forgiven their past sins against him.

> ✦ Joseph lives to see his great grandchildren. Then, after assuring his family that God will eventually bring them back to Canaan, he dies.

> ✦ Joseph's body is embalmed. Much later, it will be carried to Canaan.

We come now to the end of the Lord's glorification as shown through Genesis. In this final chapter in Genesis, we will learn of a great farewell for Israel, a final reconciliation between Joseph and his brothers, and the golden old age and death of Joseph. In the New Testament, the parallel story includes the Lord's last temptation on the cross, His states of love and compassion as His temptation ends, and His death and glorification. The Lord's states of love and compassion on the cross are depicted in the internal sense of the final experiences of Joseph's old age.

"**And Joseph fell upon his father's face, and wept on him, and kissed him**" (Gen. 50:1). **Joseph mourned and felt anguish at his father's death. He had Israel embalmed. Then followed a long period of mourning, both for Israel's family and for the Egyptians. "And the Egyptians wept for Israel for seventy days"** (Gen. 50:3).

After this period of mourning, Joseph asked Pharaoh's permission to take Israel's body to Canaan to be buried in the cave of Machpelah, as Israel had requested.

"**And Pharaoh said, 'Go up and bury your father, as he made you swear on oath.' And Joseph went to bury his father; and there went up with him all Pharaoh's servants, the elders of his house, and all the elders of the land of Egypt. And the whole house of Joseph, and his brothers, and his father's house; only their young children, and their flocks, and their herds they left in the land of Goshen.**

"**And there went up with him both chariots and horsemen; it was an extremely large army. And they came to the threshing-floor of Atad, which is at the crossing of the Jordan, and wailed there with a great and extremely loud wailing; and Joseph made a mourning for his father seven days. And the inhabitants of the land, the Canaanites, saw the mourning at the threshing-floor of Atad, and they said, 'This is an intense mourning for the Egyptians'; therefore they called the name of it Abel Mizraim, which is at the crossing of the Jordan. And Israel's sons did for him thus, as he had commanded them**" (Gen. 50:6-12).

Israel symbolizes a general goodness in the natural, and now, with his death, this goodness is glorified, made Divine. The Lord has almost completed the successive states of becoming the Divine Good (see Ath. Cr. 156, AC 4538). Jesus said in the New Testament: " 'Father, glorify your name.' Then a voice came from

heaven, saying, 'I have both glorified it and will glorify it again' "
(John 12:28). At this point in the Genesis series, the Lord has
become the Divine good or love as to the whole natural, except its
outmost parts.

What is left to be glorified in Jesus is the celestial of the spiritual (Joseph) which is the Lord's burning love for the salvation of
humankind. Also, His outer sensation and His body have yet to be
fully purified.

The hells still have access to the Lord despite the fact that He
has now become Divine Good or Love on His natural level. His
senses and body are still finite, and in those levels His finite maternal human heredity still has its awful foothold. This is seen in the
Lord's lament on the cross: "My God, My God, why have You forsaken Me?" (Matt. 27:46) His cry comes not from His Divinity but
from His finite human essence, which is still feeling separated from
His Soul. In the extreme of this final temptation, He feels He cannot save humankind. Through seeing the evil heredity operating in
His own senses, He is aware of the evil in our senses. Then all the
hells flow in together when He is in agony on the cross and infuse
the belief that humankind, in its perverted sensuous, is too evil to
be saved.

We cannot comprehend how awful this temptation is for the
Lord. It attacks Him where He is still vulnerable and devastates His
love. He realizes, I believe, that in this battle the Divine Good now
present in His natural level (Israel) is insufficient to save
humankind in these sensory-level temptations.

The great mourning procession that escorts Israel's body out of
Egypt and up to Canaan represents an intense mourning that there
is not yet a goodness in Jesus powerful enough to save humankind,
not in His last temptations that include the celestial (Joseph) and the
senses (the Egyptians here). Something is still needed, desperately.
**The procession came "to the threshing-floor of Atad, which is at
the crossing of the Jordan, and wailed there with a great and**

**extremely loud wailing" (Gen. 50:10). "And the inhabitants of
the land said, 'This is an intense mourning for the Egyptians' "
(Gen. 50:11).**

The Lord on the cross, in the depth of His last temptation,
knows that He still lacks that final quality which can save
humankind. He lacks Divinity on the plane of the senses and His
body. If He is to save us in our worst trials, when inmost love and
the body are both in despair, He has to take another and final great
step. He has to give up what is finite: He has to be transformed, glorified, even as to His senses and His body.

But before this happens, He experiences the utter devastation of
His final temptation. He sees that in *our* senses and bodies rest the
hereditary evils that would defeat us. Here, in the last stages of
regeneration, is where we would fail. He not only sees this: He *feels*
it to the very core of the Joseph within Him, the very core of His
celestial but finite love of us. This agony is given a voice at the
threshing floor of Atad at the Jordan. **For there there was a "great
and extremely loud wailing" (Gen. 50:10), an "intense mourning" (v. 11).**

The threshing-floor is the good of love (AC 7377: 4) in the Lord
(Joseph) which is in agony regarding the ultimate evils in
humankind. This wailing happens at the Jordan, the ultimate
boundary of Canaan. The Egyptians too witnessed a terrible sadness, an "intense mourning" (Gen. 50:11).

The temptation focuses on the outmost level of the Lord's mind,
and in our regeneration on the outermost of our minds. The
Egyptians here represent the sensory level, home of both sensory
knowledges and sensory delights. Here is where we would fail. The
hells force this reality into the Lord's suffering heart and mind. He
knows there is still one great and terrible step to take. His finite
human essence needs to be yielded up and glorified. To have this
happen, He must endure the agony of this temptation to its end. The
Lord foresees this in the Garden of Gethsemane: "O My Father, if

this cup cannot pass away from Me unless I drink it, Your will be done" (Matt. 26:42). During the agony of the temptation on the cross, He longs for the inmost truth that would lead to our salvation. He cries, "I thirst" (John 19:28), for water represents the living truth that can save us.

But the Lord's states on the cross are not all ones of agony and despair. He also feels a new hope, one flowing powerfully into Him from His very Soul. He foresees not final defeat, but something far different. Even on the cross, He thinks from celestial love, love that looks to our salvation. For those who put Him on the cross, He says, "Father, forgive them, for they do not know what they do" (Luke 23:34). To Mary He says, looking at John the disciple: "Woman, behold your son!" (John 19:26). Then He says to the disciple, "Behold your mother!" (John 19:27). And to the good thief Jesus says words of comfort: "Assuredly, I say to you, today you will be with Me in Paradise" (Luke 23:43).

These words of compassion, spoken even while on the cross, show how much He loves us and how near to us He is. This has its counterpart in the story of Joseph. After Israel was buried in the cave of Machpelah, there seems to be, representatively, a change of state.

"Joseph returned to Egypt, he and his brothers, and all who went up with him to bury his father. . . .And Joseph's brothers saw that their father had died, and they said, 'Perhaps Joseph will hate us and will fully return to us all the evil with which we repaid him.' And they gave a command to Joseph, saying, 'Your father commanded before he died, saying, "Thus you are to say to Joseph, I beg you, forgive — I beg you — the transgressions of your brothers, and their sin, for the evil with which they repaid you, and now forgive, I beg you, the transgressions of the servants of your father's God" ' " (Gen. 50:15-17, selections).

"And Joseph wept as they spoke to him" (Gen. 50:17).

"And his brothers also went and fell down before him, and said, 'Behold, we are your slaves.' And Joseph said to them, 'Do

not be afraid, for am I in the place of God? And you thought evil against me; God thought (to turn) it into good, in order to do what is in accord with this day, to bestow life on a great people. And now, do not be afraid. I will sustain you and your young children.' And Joseph consoled them, and spoke to their heart" (Gen. 50:18-21).

"And Joseph spoke to their heart." The Lord does the same on the cross to those who are there, both those who love Him and those who crucified Him. He becomes reconciled with those near Him who will listen. So Joseph becomes reconciled with His brothers after returning to Egypt. Joseph forgave them, as Jesus forgives even those who crucified Him.

In the Joseph story, and in the New Testament pre-Easter and Easter stories, the Lord "speaks to [our] heart." He testifies of His love and His willingness to forgive.

That this happened in Joseph's life after his return to Egypt indicates that the states of conclusion after Israel's burial focus on the sensuous, for this outmost level is now being glorified. On the cross, the Lord's temptations have their ultimates in His physical pain and eventually in His physical death.

However, toward the end of His time on the cross, Jesus Christ experiences integrations and elevations of state. The Joseph story represented this in his final time in Egypt, before he died. **He lived to "a hundred and ten years" (Gen. 50:22).** This signifies a full state of remains or states of innocence, and a unifying of the Divine remains in the Lord.

"The Divine remains which pertained to the Lord were all the Divine states which He procured for Himself, and by means of which He united the Human Essence to the Divine Essence. These cannot be compared to the remains that pertain to a person, for the latter are human, not Divine" (AC 1906:4).

"And Joseph saw Ephraim's sons of the third generation; also the sons of Machir, Manasseh's son, were born on Joseph's knees" (Gen. 50:23). With us, Ephraim and Manasseh are the new understanding and new will in the sensuous. With the Lord, they are the glorifying of His sensuous level, of His understanding and will on this ultimate level.

"And Joseph said to his brothers, 'I am dying, and God will certainly visit you and cause you to go up out of this land to the land which He swore to Abraham, Isaac, and Jacob.' And Joseph made the children of Israel swear, saying, 'God will certainly visit you, and you shall cause my bones to go up from here.' And Joseph died, a hundred and ten years old; and they embalmed him, and he was put in an ark in Egypt" (Gen. 50:24-26).

When Joseph dies, it is the symbolic picture of the end and fulfillment of the glorification. The Lord's former sensuous then is put aside, and He assumes a new Sensuous level and Body that are Divine! In this transformation is the greatest miracle in history. This is symbolized by **the embalming of Joseph and then later the taking up of his body and its being carried back to the land of Canaan.** Symbolically, Joseph returned home at last. The land of Canaan represents heaven, and in the highest sense it represents the Lord in His glorified Divine Human. Joseph's dying means spiritually a whole new beginning for humankind. The celestial of the spiritual, Jesus' finite but wonderful love for our salvation, becomes glorified: it becomes *Divine*. He returns Home, One with His Father.

This happens with His victory and death on the cross. He says, speaking His last words in His earthly body: "Father, into Your hands I commend My spirit" (Luke 23:46). Then in those words that mark the completion of the glorification: "It is finished" (John 19: 30). The finite human essence has achieved its inmost goal, and now is replaced by the Divine Human in its fullness.

What is not shown in the Joseph story in representative terms is

255

the glorification of the Lord's body in the tomb, although **Joseph did ask his sons to bring back "my bones" to the land of Canaan (Gen. 50:25),** and Canaan with Jesus signifies the Divine. We read that **Joseph was "embalmed, and he was put in an ark in Egypt" (Gen. 50:26).** This means preservation of his body from any corruption by evil (see AC 6595). But in the celestial sense, this is to be understood in a "supereminent sense" (AC 10252:7). In this sense, it stands for the dissipation of the finite human body that was born of Mary, followed by the rising of the glorified Divine Body itself (*Ibid.*). This is the Divine resurrection of Jesus Christ. He is indeed brought to the Divine, to the Divine Canaan.

It is interesting that when Jesus dies, His body is buried in the tomb of Joseph of Arimathea (Matt. 27: 57-60). The name "Joseph" catches the eye. It is perhaps one of the final correlations of Joseph's Genesis story with that of Jesus in the New Testament.

Seen from the reality of eternal life, Joseph's story has a golden ending. He lived out his final years in Goshen, a portion of Egypt, surrounded by family who loved him. He saw his children and their children even to the third generation. He was loved by his own family and highly respected by the Egyptians. His dreams as a seventeen-year-old came true: his family did bow down before him, but out of love, not because of any domination by him. Even the coat of many colors was representatively restored to him. For the celestial love clothes itself with all the arts and sciences of creation, and these bring bright colors to its innocence.

Once Joseph dies, then, in representatives, Jesus' finite human essence is gone – replaced by His glorified Divine Human! Yet Joseph's meaning is not lost; it is replaced by the Divine Human, Who now Divinely loves humankind and its salvation. And His name is called "Wonderful." Jesus has become the Divine Good on every plane, from inmosts to outmosts. From this good proceeds healing Divine Truth (AC 9670, Ath. Cr. 156).

It is to the New Testament that we must turn to see clearly the Lord in His Easter rising and in His post-Easter times with His disciples.

"Now after the Sabbath, as the first day of the week began to dawn, Mary Magdalene and the other Mary came to see the tomb. And behold there was a great earthquake; for an angel of the Lord descended from heaven, and came and rolled back the stone from the door, and sat on it. His countenance was like lightning, and his clothing as white as snow. . . .The angel answered and said to the women, 'Do not be afraid, for I know that you seek Jesus Who was crucified. He is not here; for He is risen, as He said. Come, see the place where the Lord lay' " (Matt. 28:1-6, selections).

Mary Magdalene runs to Peter and John and tells them what has happened. They run to the tomb and find the clothes in which Jesus' body had been wrapped, but Him they do not find.

"But Mary stood outside by the tomb, weeping, and as she wept she stooped down, and looked into the tomb. And she saw two angels in white sitting, one at the head and the other at the feet where the body of Jesus had lain. Then they said to her, 'Woman, why are you weeping?' She said to them, 'Because they have taken away my Lord, and I do not know where they have laid Him.' Now when she had said this, she turned around and saw Jesus standing there, and did not know that it was Jesus.

"Jesus said to her, 'Woman, why are you weeping? Whom are you seeking?' She, supposing Him to be the gardener, said to Him, 'Sir, if you have carried Him away, tell me where You have laid Him, and I will take Him away.' Jesus said to her, 'Mary.' She turned and said to Him, 'Rabboni!' " (John 20:11-17).

In a sense, each of us is Mary Magdalene. We have sinned in

our lives, yet we search for the Lord. The message of Easter is that He is not in the tomb, "He is risen." To each of us He would come and say our spiritual name. He waits for us to discover Him.

It is in the *Arcana* story of Abraham, Isaac, Jacob and Joseph that the Lord makes Himself visible to our hearts and thoughts, to our emotions and natural ideas. In the glorification story disclosed there He reveals His inner nature as He never has before. He speaks to our hearts and minds. He shows, step by step, how He made a path for us: a path to heaven.

"The Lord's life in the world was an example according to which the people of the church are to live, as the Lord Himself teaches in John: 'I have given to you an example, that you also should do as I have done to you. If you know these things, blessed are you if you do them' " (John 13:15,17; AE 254:2).

He shows us The Path. He founded it and then re-established it on earth. He invites us to take this spiritual highway and gradually, step by step, to come to Him. He reveals to us what He thought and felt in His own glorification: His joys and insights, His awful temptations, His liberating victories. We do not lose Him when He is glorified. We find Him.

The Lord says to us, "Peace be with you" (John 20:19).

"Our Father, Who art in the heavens, hallowed be Thy name. Thy kingdom come. Thy will be done, as in heaven so upon the earth. Give us this day our daily bread. And forgive us our debts as we forgive our debtors. And lead us not into temptation, but deliver us from evil. For Thine is the kingdom, and the power, and the glory forever." Amen.

ABOUT THE AUTHOR

Geoffrey S. Childs is also author of *The Golden Thread* (1986, General Church Press). He was ordained into the ministry of the General Church of the New Jerusalem in 1952, and since then has served as pastor in various cities in the United States, Canada, and South Africa, as well as serving as President of the Academy of the New Church from 1987 to 1992. Mr. Childs now lives with Helga, his wife of fifty years, in Bryn Athyn, Pennsylvania. They have eight grown children.

ABOUT THE COVER ART AND ARTIST

Kären Childs Elder is the sixth child of Geoffrey and Helga. She graduated from the Ontario College of Art in 1981 with a degree in fine arts, and now lives with her husband Jack and their six children in Rochester, Michigan. She also writes and performs spiritual music, available through Fountain Publishing.

The cover painting that Kären created for *The Path* depicts two layers of meaning from Genesis, chapter 15. In the background, Abram gazes up at the sky as Jehovah promises that his descendants will be as numerous as the stars. In the foreground, young Jesus gazes upon a vision, in which His Divine Soul promises that the number of people He will save will be as numerous as the stars.